Museums in Budapest

Museums in Budapest

Hungarian National Museum

Museum of Fine Arts

Hungarian National Gallery

Museum of Applied Arts

Ethnographical Museum

Budapest Historical Museum

CORVINA

Title of the original:
Budapest múzeumai, Corvina Kiadó, Budapest, 1984
Translated by Maria Steiner
Translation revised by Margaret Davies
Design by János Lengyel

Colour photographs by
Bakos, Ágnes: 142–148
Gábler, Csaba: 77, 90, 91, 95
Gottl, Egon: 80, 98
Gyarmathy, László: 39, 81, 83, 88, 89, 123, 127
Hász, András: 103, 113
Kolozs, Ágnes: 74, 78, 79, 84, 85, 92, 93, 96, 97
Kovács, Kornél: 94
Milos, József: 99
Molnár, Ilona: 124, 125
Pelbárt, János: 57, 72
Schiller, Alfréd sen.: 32, 52, 54–56, 60, 61
Schiller, Alfréd: 29, 33, 47, 51, 53, 62, 63, 65–68, 70, 71, 100–102,
    104–112, 114–116, 118–122
Szelényi, Károly: 1–25, 30, 31, 34–38, 40–46, 48, 49, 69, 76, 82,
    117
Szepsy Szűcs, Levente: 50
Tihanyi, Bence: 126, 128–139, 141

Black-and-white photographs by
Bakos, Ágnes: 140
Bokor, Zsuzsa: 58, 59, 64
Kolozs, Ágnes: 73, 75, 86, 87
Szenczi, Mária: 26, 27, 28

CONTENTS

Second edition

© Heir of Ferenc Fülep, Marianna Haraszti-Takács, Zsuzsa Turcsány,
Piroska Weiner, János Kodolányi, heir of Miklós Horváth

ISBN 963 13 2756 6
Printed in Hungary, 1989
Athenaeum Printing House, Budapest
CO 2736-h-8993

Hungarian National Museum

The Hungarian National Museum was founded in 1802. All over Europe, including Hungary, the ideas of the French Enlightenment persuaded some aristocrats to open their private collections to the public. In Hungary, the foundation of the National Museum was aided by yet another factor: the centuries of Habsburg rule had given rise to a strong national reaction, which sparked off a struggle to have Hungarian declared the official language, and a proper esteem accorded to the relics of the Hungarian historical past; the movement became finally embodied in the foundation of the National Museum and the Academy of Sciences.

The establishment of the National Museum is linked with the name of Count Ferenc Széchényi, a talented aristocrat of European learning of the turn of the eighteenth and nineteenth centuries, who by the end of the eighteenth century had already succeeded in raising his family library and various collections to a status of national magnitude, and from 1786 onwards, considered them the basis for a "national library". The foundations for his collection of coins and antiquities were Roman coins from Sirmium, while for his library he collected specifically Hungarian material and works with Hungarian connections. In his deed of foundation of 25 November 1802, by which he officially donated his collections to the nation, he stipulated that the library be called *Bibliotheca Hungarica Familiae Comitum Széchényi Patriae sacrata*, and the Hungarian National Library has retained that name ever since. At the time of the foundation, the collection consisted of 11,884 prints, 1,150 manuscripts, 142 volumes of maps and engravings and 2,019 coats of arms. In 1807, it was enlarged by 2,675 coins, antiquities and a few pictures listed in the inventory *Catalogus Nummorum Hungariae*. Article No. 24 of the 1807 statute accepted the material into the nation's possession. The memory of the founder is preserved by his statue standing in the garden of the Museum.

By 1804 the library was opened to research workers. In 1814 the Department of Coins and Antiquities became independent, and in 1825, issued its first catalogue entitled *Cimeliotheca Musei Nationalis*. During the following years the National Museum expanded its holdings considerably through purchases and presents.

The collection was first housed in the former priory of the Order of St Paul in Pest. The institution was directly supervised by the vice-regent, the Palatine Archduke Joseph, who managed the affairs of the Museum with great care and solicitude. One of the conditions for further expansion was the acquisition of an adequate building. As early as 1807 the Palatine Joseph commissioned the Pest architect József Hild to prepare designs for a building for the National Museum, but at the time the plans could not be executed as the ground purchased for the purpose was found to be too small and exposed to the risk of fire. Finally, by exchanging the plot, they acquired the present ground of the Hungarian National Museum. But construction work was not commenced for quite some time, and the cause of the National Museum was only taken up again by the National Assembly in 1836, which allocated the necessary building costs. The Palatine Joseph commissioned the Pest architect Mihály Pollack to design the building, and on 28 December 1836 a contract was signed with him. Construction work began on 22 June 1837, but the great flood that destroyed the city of Pest in 1838, interrupted the work. The edifice was completed by July 1847, after ten years of work. The façade is 109 metres long, with a 34.7 metres wide, eight-column portico. The tympanum above the columns shows a group of figures by the Munich sculptor Raffael Monti, with the female figure of Pannonia in the centre, flanked by the allegorical figures of Science and Art on the right, and of History and Fame on the left. Early in 1848, all the collections were put on display in the newly completed building.

The building of the Museum played a major role in the events of the 1848 Revolution. The demonstrations by the youth and populace of Pest took place in the garden of the Museum, and the Upper House of the National Assembly met in its assembly hall.

The crushing of the War of Independence in 1849 was followed by hard times. Heavy taxes were levied on the Museum and they wanted to take its contents to Vienna. But in the years after the War of Independence, the general public once again took up the cause of the National Museum. Its garden was planted following an initiative by the Hungarian Women's Society. Fund-raising concerts were held in the assembly hall, several of which were conducted by Ferenc Erkel and, in 1858, by Ferenc Liszt. As a result of negligence on the part of the government, the museum building fell into a state of poor repair, the expansion of the collections came to a halt, and its Gallery was the only section to be enriched by some valuable pieces. The situation improved after the agreement known as the *Ausgleich* or Compromise between the nation and the Habsburg house in 1867. The Museum was allocated a regular budget, the library and the exhibition rooms were properly equipped, steam-heating was installed and the vestibule was decorated with paintings by Károly Lotz and Mór Than. But from 1870 to 1902 the government used the assembly hall as the session room of the Upper House. Ferenc Pulszky became the director of the Museum, and the Department of Antiquities was headed by Flóris Rómer and József Hampel, whose activity raised the Museum to the best European standards. As a result of their work of organization, the rescuing of antiquities became a nationwide concern. Mainly at Flóris Rómer's initiative, museums and museum societies sprang up one after the other throughout the country. In 1867, the Museum's archaeological material was displayed at the World Exhibition in Paris, and as a result, in 1876 the 8th International Anthropological and Archaeological Congress was held in Budapest. The major archaeological finds of the country were also exhibited on the occasion.

In the 1870s the enlargement of the collections began a process during which certain great specialized museums branched off from the National Museum. In 1871, the state purchased the largest aristocratic gallery, the Esterházy collection, and founded the National Gallery, which alongside the Esterházy collection includes the Pyrker Gallery, which was presented to the Museum in 1836, and Arnold Ipolyi's collection. The merger of the National Gallery with the National Museum's Gallery led to the setting up of the Museum of Fine Arts, the foundation of which was the subject of an Act passed in 1896. The Hungarian Historical Gallery was set up in 1884; it was later annexed to the Museum of Fine Arts, but since 1934 has formed part of the National Museum.

In 1872, an independent Ethnographical Department was set up within the Museum, headed by János Xantus, who enriched the Museum's collections with considerable material from overseas; later Ottó Herman and János Jankó won permanent renown by collecting Hungarian ethnographical material. After several temporary locations, in 1925 the ethnographical collection was given a building of its own, but continued to function within the framework of the National Museum up till 1947, when it gained independence.

In 1878 the Museum of Applied Arts grew into an independent unit out of the National Museum's Collection of Handicrafts; in 1885 its material was separated from that of the Department of Antiquities, and in 1890 it was decided to construct a separate building for it in Üllői út.

The Natural History Museum was also set up within the framework of the National Museum. It was established by Julianna Festetics, the wife of Ferenc Széchényi, the founder of the National Museum. In 1808, Julianna Festetics also donated her rich collection of minerals to the National Museum. In 1870, three independent departments were set up within the National Museum: the Mineralogy, the Botany and the Zoology Departments. The independent Natural History Museum was established in 1933.

The Széchényi Library and the Hungarian National Museum were under joint management until 1949, when the two institutions were divided. Today the National Museum houses the country's archaeological, numismatic and historical collections.

During the Second World War the building suffered 75 hits during air raids; the roof, doors and windows were all destroyed, and the collections suffered severe damage. One of the store-rooms, filled with furniture, carpets and goldsmith's works, was totally burned down. But despite the serious losses, the Museum soon recuperated, and in 1948, nearly a million people went to see the first great post-war exhibition to commemorate the centenary of the 1848 Revolution and War of Independence. By 1952 the renovation of the building was completed, but during the 1956 counter-revolution it again suffered grave damage.

The 1960s and '70s saw the accomplishment of the Museum's scholarly and cultural activities and organizational consolidation. Large-scale excavations were started in connection with the construction work of the Danube hydroelectric station; the research staff of the Museum published many outstanding works; a new, great archaeological exhibition was opened, and there was a considerable increase in the number of visitors. The institution celebrated the 175th anniversary of its foundation in 1977. To mark the occasion, the Presidential Council of the Hungarian People's Republic conferred the Red Banner Medal of Labour on the Museum. In January 1978, the Hungarian crown and royal insignia, which at the end of the Second World War had been taken out of the country, were returned to Hungary. They have been displayed at a temporary exhibition in the National Museum. Since their return in 1978, the coronation regalia have been visited by more than four million people.

Today the National Museum has two great permanent exhibitions. One presents the major archaeological relics of the country from the Palaeolithic period until the time of the Hungarian Conquest at the end of the ninth century. The exhibition was opened in 1977, as the most modern display ever to have been mounted within the walls of the Museum, which has once again brought the National Museum up to the highest standards in Europe as far as exhibitions are concerned.

The other display presents the most important events in the history of the country and its people from the Migration Period to the mid-nineteenth century. The exhibition was opened in 1967 and includes the most valuable relics of Hungarian history, the most beautiful pieces of Romanesque, Gothic and Renaissance architecture and the most outstanding works of the material and intellectual culture, art and literature of each period. A new dimension has been added by the various tools, utensils and equipment which have come from excavations of villages that were destroyed in the Middle Ages, and which give an insight into the daily life of the people. Several museums and church collections have loaned materials for the exhibition, which employs a truly complex method of presentation.

In keeping with tradition, concerts have frequently been held before large audiences in the Museum's assembly hall, often with noted artists performing on the Museum's restored historical musical instruments. Since 1978, when the exhibition of the Hungarian crown and coronation regalia was mounted in the assembly hall, concerts have been held in the rooms of the historical exhibition.

The National Museum has four institutions in the countryside: an open-air archaeological museum at Vértesszőlős, where in 1965 a fragment of the skull of prehistoric man (*Homo sapiens palaeohungaricus*) dating from some 300,000 to 400,000 years ago was found together with traces of a one-time settlement; the excavated ruins of King Matthias Corvinus's Renaissance palace and the adjoining museum at Visegrád; the Rákóczi Castle and museum at Sárospatak, and the memorial museum in Lajos Kossuth's house of birth at Monok.

The publications of the National Museum include *Folia Archaeologica* and *Folia Historica* (the Museum's annual reports); *Régészeti Füzetek* (Archaeological Papers), Series I and II; *Dunai Régészeti Híradó* (Danube Archaeological Journal); periodical publications, e.g. *The Hungarian National Museum* (Corvina Press, Budapest, 1977), issued on the 175th anniversary of the Museum; exhibition catalogues, guides, folding albums and pamphlets. Major studies and monographs by members of the staff of the Museum are published by the Hungarian Academy of Sciences.

In its inner organizational structure the Museum has more or less preserved its traditional arrangement. Today it has the following departments:

DEPARTMENT OF ARCHAEOLOGY. The sphere of the Department's collection includes finds ranging from the Palaeolithic period to the late ninth century (only from the territory of Hungary). According to statistics available in 1981, the Department holds 571,359 items, divided into five major groups, with the material from Palaeolithic, prehistoric and Roman times and the Migration Period totalling at 499,190 pieces, and the collection of animal bones amounting to 72,169.

The rich collections of the Department include a number of outstanding objects of international significance. The Palaeolithic collection preserves, among other things, the fragment of the skull of the Vértesszőlős prehistoric man which has been mentioned already, and which is one of the oldest hominid remains in Europe. Reference should be made to the mining implements from the Lovas paint mine (40,000 B.C.). Important pieces of the collection are the urns from Center, the cart-vessels from Budakalász and Sziget-szentmárton, the Hallstatt culture gold hoard from Fokoru and Angyalföld, the Etruscan type bronze cists from Kurd and the Scythian gold stags. Outstanding pieces of the Roman collection include a silver tripod from Polgárdi, the cart finds from Somodor, the bronze law tablet from Ószőny, the early Christian sarcophagus from Szekszárd with a glass vessel with reticulated ornament *(vas diatretum)*, the ivory Bacchus statuette from Szombathely and the gilded bronze bust of Emperor Valentinian II. The collection of the Migration Period includes some objects which are outstanding by any international criterion, such as the Hunnish princely finds of Szeged–Nagyszéksós, the second gold hoard of Szilágysom-lyó (now Şimleu Silvaniei, Rumania), the German gold find of Bakodpuszta and the Avar princely finds coming from various sites (Bócsa, Ozora, Kunágota, etc.).

MEDIEVAL DEPARTMENT. The scope of the Department's collections covers relics dating from the tenth century to the end of the sixteenth century. According to statistics available in 1981, the number of items amounts to 68,267.

A major place in the collection is occupied by the finds of the first Magyar settlers of Hungary, and within that the silver sabretache plates and silver dress ornaments attest a high level of metal craftsmanship. They also include the crown originating from the Byzantine Emperor Constantine IX Monomachus; a centaur-shaped aquamanile, the belt buckle from Kígyóspuszta, enamelled bowls from Limoges, the grave goods of the Hungarian King Béla III and his wife, the fifteenth-century library chest from Bártfa (now Bardejov, Czechoslovakia), the glass goblet of King Matthias Corvinus, the Renaissance pew of the Nyírbátor church, a sixteenth-century Turkish officer's leather cloak, the enamelled gold goblet of Prince György Rákóczi I of Transylvania, the Rákóczi–Erdődy treasures, etc.

DEPARTMENT OF MODERN TIMES. Basically, the sphere of the Department's collection ranges from the eighteenth century to the present day, and the collection of objects from recent times has become considerably increased in the last decade. The Department also encompasses a number of special groups of collections: weapons, goldsmith's work, textiles, furniture, ceramics, musical instruments and other miscellaneous materials. In 1981 the number of items came to 45,946. They include many outstanding objects of international interest, such as the throne tapestry of King Matthias Corvinus, which were woven in Florence, the wedding garments of the Hungarian King Louis II and his wife, the dress of the Transylvanian Princess Catherine of Brandenburg, and Hungarian minor aristocratic and folk embroideries. Of the pieces of furniture particular mention should be made of the suite with Gobelin upholstery from the Regéc castle of the Rákóczi family; the musical instruments include Mozart's clavichord, the Esterházy barytone, Marie Antoinette's harp and Beethoven's piano; the collection of weapons proudly includes the sword of King Wladislas II sent to him by the Pope and the ornamental weapons of Transylvanian princes, while outstanding among goldsmith's works are the chess-board of Prince Mihály Apafi I of Transylvania and the gold dinner-table set of Maria Theresa.

DEPARTMENT OF COINS AND MEDALS. The most important collections of the Department are the antique materials which include Greek and Roman coins and coins of Celtic tribes minted after Greek and Roman models, the Hungarian collection (up to the present day), and commemorative medals, plaques and badges. Some of the noteworthy pieces of the Department include Roman gold bars from Kraszna (now Crasna, Rumania), gold *solidi* (fifth century) from Szikáncs, *denarii* of the Hungarian King Stephen I, gold pieces of 100 and 50 ducats of Mihály Apafi I, the eighteenth-century St George gold coin weighing 100 ducats, minted at Körmöcbánya (now Kremnica, Czechoslovakia), the badge and collar of the Order of the Golden Fleece (nineteenth century), etc. In 1981, the collection numbered 288,944 items.

HISTORICAL GALLERY. The collection of the Gallery includes portraits, engravings and drawings of historical interest, and more recently photographs as well. Pictures of special interest are the portrait of the Transylvanian Prince Ferenc Rákóczi II by Ádám Mányoki (1703), and Miklós Barabás's drawings of Hungarian generals of the War of Independence in 1848–49. In 1981 the collection consisted of 58,746 items.

DOCUMENTATION DEPARTMENT. It was set up in 1952 to store the documentation of all archaeological excavations going on in the country, and the negatives and photographs of the objects in the Museum. The records on all excavations in Hungary are collected here and are published by the Department every year in Series I of *Régészeti Füzetek*. In 1981 the collected material amounted to 79,235 items.

ARCHAEOLOGICAL LIBRARY. The Library was established in 1952, with its main scope of activity covering the collection of works on archaeology, numismatics and history. It stocks 101,724 works and periodicals, and is one of the most important specialized libraries in Central Europe.

The restoration workshops are responsible for the preservation of the huge material. The Public Education Group, set up a few years ago, also carries on a comprehensive programme.

Ferenc Fülep

DESCRIPTION
OF ILLUSTRATIONS

1 Urns from Center
20th century B.C. Found in 1958, during excavations of a graveyard, as part of one grave furniture.
(a) Big Greyish-Brown Urn
Height: 48.4 cm; length of head: 21.1 cm; diameter of base: 17.5 cm
(b) Smaller Urn, with Light and Dark Grey Spots
Height: 40.6 cm; diameters: mouth: 15 cm; base: 17.5 cm
(c) Small Urn. Dark Grey, in Places Restored.
Height: 23.9 cm; length of head: 12.6 cm; diameter of base: 9.1 cm
The three vessels are outstanding works of late Copper Age pottery. The human figures are represented in an extremely simplified manner. The urns might have been used in the religious cults of the time. Their closest parallels have been found in Troy.

2 Cart Vessel from Budakalász
End of third millennium B.C. Height: 8 cm; length: 11 cm. Found in one of the graves of the Baden culture at Budakalász in 1952.
The body consists of a square wickerwork type cart, with its four solid disc-wheels forming the foot of the vessel. The handle symbolizes the cart pole, which originally rose high above the rim (now broken). The lengthwise parallel lines in a square frame at the bottom of the vessel indicate the planks of the cart. The vessel is made of clay, painted red inside and outside. This type of cart was probably developed in Mesopotamia, from where it reached Europe. The Budakalász cart provides important data on the life of the stock-breeding people of the Baden culture, the use of draught animals and the development of the cart in Europe.

3 Scythian Gold Stags
(a) Gold Stag from Zöldhalompuszta. Gold.
Mutilated length: 37 cm. The object was found accidentally in 1928.

The stag is portrayed at the moment of collapse, the head looking back, the antlers reaching forward, with the head of a hook-billed bird between its neck and antler. The back side of the legs, the tail and the head are ornamented with thick braiding. It is a repoussé work. The eyes and ears are filled with pale blue glass-paste. The finders cut the object up to pieces and it has survived in that mutilated state.
(b) Gold Stag from Tápiószentmárton. Electrum.
Height: 22.7 cm. Found during excavations in 1923.
The stag bends its antler backwards, and draws its leg under its body. The antler consists of two protruding tines and four tines tilting backwards in an S shape. Some of the branches are accentuated by strong punched lines. The fore-haunch, the neck, the middle line of the triple eyebrow and the hindquarters have punched borders, and the rest of the lines have braided borders. The neck consists of two converging flat plates. The legs are thickset, much too short and robust when compared with the body.

The two gold stags are fine examples of Scythian art, which developed along the northern littoral of the Black Sea. The technique is reminiscent of wood-carving. The age of the Zöldhalompuszta gold stag may be dated to the second half of the sixth century B.C., while the one from Tápiószentmárton was made somewhat later.

4 Bronze Jug and Patera
Ist century B.C. Found in 1831 during earth works at Egyed.
(a) Jug. Height: 24.3 cm
The rim of the lip of the jug is decorated with a row-of-eggs pattern, the neck with vine scrolls. The shoulder has a cyma moulding running all round, and under a strip of double scroll-work a sequence of Egyptian deities represents a procession of the god Isis. Below the frieze are more foliate ornaments, with a heart-shaped palmette line round the foot. The scrolls and leaves on the

neck are of silver, the clusters of gold, and the figures are also outlined by gold threads.

(b) Patera. Length: 34 cm; Diameter of the plate: 23.4 cm

The handle is cast in bronze, the plate is made of copper. The handle is richly ornamented. The outside of the plate is undecorated, the edge of the inside is covered with scroll-work and two rows of acanthus leaves, while the middle picture on the patera shows a Nile scene with a hippopotamus, a crocodile and water fowl.

5 Glass Cup with Reticulated Ornament (vas diatretum)

Found in 1845 in an ornate early Christian sarcophagus at Szekszárd. It was presumably made in Cologne and came to Pannonia by trade in the early 4th century A.D. Height: 12 cm

A blue-white, cup-shaped glass vessel, with a Greek inscription in protruding letters running round its side: "Make offerings to the shepherd, drink, and you shall live". Under the legend is a protruding, reticulated collar, which corresponds in its material with those of the cup and the Greek letters. Soldered to the bottom of the cup were snails and fish made of blown glass serving as the foot. Based on the inscription it can be ranked among early Christian relics in Pannonia.

6 Late Roman Ornate Helmet

Found in the Danube in 1898, during the construction work of Elizabeth Bridge. Height: 13 cm; longitudinal diameter: 24 cm; width: 17 cm

The helmet, presumably having belonged to a high-ranking officer, came from the advanced counter-fortress on the left bank of the Danube and might have been made in the second half of the fourth century A.D. The iron helmet was covered with silver-gilt plates. A low crest reaches down from the mid-front to the nape. The rim ends at the bottom in figural ornaments. Besides embossed punched ornaments, geometrical designs also feature on the helmet, wich from the outside is embellished with semi-precious stones set in cells with punched borders (green, white striped lilac and opalescent).

7 Gold Brooches

From the second Szilágysomlyó (now Şimleul Silvaniei, Rumania) hoard. The brooches were made in the Pontus region in the late 4th and early 5th centuries, and found in 1899 during agricultural work.

(a) Onyx Gold Brooch. Length: 17.1 cm; largest width: 11.4 cm

The head consists of an octagonal, 7 cm long cross-bar with onion-shaped gold knobs at the two ends and in the middle. Above the middle knob is a reddish-brown, convex piece of glass in a frame and at the two sides there is a hemispherical rock-crystal also framed. The bow consists of an oval gold plate to hold the onyx. The eight gold cells embedded along the edge of the finely polished onyx are set with red stones. The onyx is framed with a band of *cloisonné* work set with red, green and white stones (several of which have fallen out).

The leg consists of a hexagonal, arched member with a convex rock-crystal at the end. Two cornelians and a green glass plate are embedded in three cells (one of the cornelians is missing). The clasp for the pin is soldered to the bottom.

(b) Gold Brooch. Length (with knob): 24.8 cm

Large pair of brooches of silver with gold plating. The head is semicircular with a knob in the middle and surrounded by two rows of twisted gold wire, which enclose three circular cells divided into four sections, linked by elongated cells to the palmette with indented decoration in the middle of the bow. The interstices are filled with drop-shaped and square cells set with red stones and green glass plates. The bow is of solid silver and carries a series of cells filled with red garnets and green glass plates on its back. The back of the head shows traces of a clasp for pin.

8 Bronze Cauldron from Törtel

End of 4th century–early 5th century A.D. Height: 89 cm; diameter: 50 cm. From Törtel

A cylindrical cast bronze cauldron, rounded off at the bottom. The casting mould consisted of four pieces. There are remnants of a cylindrical foot at the bottom, now broken off. At the upper rim the two handles facing each other were cast from six bars and semicircular plates. The body of the cauldron is divided by cast bronze strips and the rim decorated with thickened ribs.

The sacrificial vessels found in Hungary belong to the same stylistic group and to the same period, having spread from the northern littoral of the Black Sea. The rock-paintings in the Minusinsk region show several variants of such bronze cauldrons. Their use may be connected with the appearance of the Huns.

9 Avar Strap-ends
(a) Late Avar bronze strap-end with a design of floral patterns. Length: 15.6 cm; width: 3.3 cm. From grave 335 of the Avar burial ground at Szebény
(b) A great strap-end in cast, gilded bronze, with a scroll and a scene of animal combat. Length: 11.8 cm; width: 3.2 cm. Hungary, unknown location
(c) Bronze great strap-end ornamented with an openwork floral scroll. Length: 13.8 cm; width: 3 cm. From Regöly
The great strap-ends are the largest mounts on Avar belts, which indicated the rank of their owners. Animal and floral ornamentations are among the characteristic motifs of nomadic art. They have been dated to the eighth century.

10 Sabretache Plate from Tarcal
10th century. Length: 13.4 cm; width: 12.4 cm. Found in 1894 in a grave, during vineyard work.
The front plate is of silver, the back one of copper; the two are riveted together with a thin silver strip that runs round the perimeter of the silver plate. The vegetal ornament is slightly protruding from the dimly gilded background.

Such plates decorated the leather sabretaches of the conquering Hungarians. The technique of plate covering was an ancient tradition in the region of Southern Russia. The motifs can be traced back to the Sassanid-Persian art.

11 Crown of Byzantine Emperor Constantine IX Monomachus
From Nyitraivánka (now Ivanka pri Nitre, Czechoslovakia)
(a) Monomachus Crown—detail, with picture of the Emperor. Length: 11.5 cm; width: 4.8 cm. Gold, with Byzantine *cloisonné* enamel ornamentation on the surface
The Hungarian National Museum possesses seven such gold plates, rectangular in shape and arched at the top. These came to light during ploughing in 1860. The detail reproduced here shows Emperor Constantine IX Monomachus. He stands on a semicircular stool in imperial robes wearing the imperial crown *(stemma)* on his head and holding a "flag with flagpost" *(labarum)* in his right hand. His footwear is purple. The Greek inscription at his head gives his name. On his left is Zoë and on his right Theodora, the two empresses, both wearing long-sleeved blue robes with wide golden collars. They hold long, sceptre-like rods in their right and left hands respectively. On either side of the empresses—on plates of gradually decreasing size—are dancers in green and in white tunics. To the right and left of these are figures representing Justice and Humility. The individual plates are bordered on two sides by enamelled scrolls of green leaves and multicoloured birds. The present form of the imperial crown is a reconstruction.

The crown was made between 1042 and 1050 in Constantinople in the imperial goldsmith's workshop there. Is was probably presented by the Byzantine court to the Hungarian King Andrew I (1046–1061).

12 The Hungarian Royal Crown
Height: 19 cm; diameter: 21.6 × 20.3 cm; outer perimeter: 68.5 cm; inner perimeter: 63.6 cm; weight: 2,056 gr
The lower and upper parts of the crown were fitted together presumably in the twelfth century, when it was given its present-day form. The gold is of different colours and presumably different standards and is decorated with *cloisonné* enamel plates, precious stones and pearls. The lower band is called the "Greek crown", as the historical per-

sons featuring on it are marked in Greek inscriptions. The upper part is called the "Latin crown" after the Latin inscriptions of the apostles depicted on it.

Above the band of the "Greek crown" the central place is filled by the figure of the enthroned Christ. The two cypresses on the right and left of His throne have Christ's monogram above them. Right and left to the central field are translucent triangular and semicircular parts. They decrease in size towards the back, and continue in pearls pierced with small rivets. The band below them is decorated with eight enamel plates; the empty fields are filled with large gems (sapphire, almandine and garnet); the band is framed by rows of pearls. The crown's lower band has nine little gold chains (*pendilia*), four hanging from both sides and one from the back, each ending in three precious stones. The order of the enamel plates is as follows: Christ, flanked on either side by Archangels Michael and Gabriel; next to them the two Byzantine warrior saints, St George and St Demetrius, followed by the two medical saints, Cosmas and Damian. The three historical personalities at the back of the crown are: opposite Christ, above the band is the Byzantine Emperor Michael VII Ducas in imperial robes, with a crown on his head and a *labarum* in his right hand, his left rests on his sword. In the lower row, to the right of the emperor is the crowned figure of Constantine Porphyrogenitus, the young co-regent. To the left of the emperor, also in the lower row, is a black bearded man with crown on his head, a sceptre-like cross in his right and with his left grasping the hilt of the sword: this is the Hungarian King Géza I. According to Byzantine protocol, the inscription of the names and ranks of the Byzantine emperor and Constantine is in red letters, while the name of the Hungarian king in bluish-black letters.

The three monarchs reigned simultaneously, between 1074 and 1077, which determines the date of origin of the enamels. From that it is clear that the lower part of the crown in that form had no connection with Hungarian King St Stephen.

The enamels are products of the goldsmith's workshop of the Byzantine court.

The "Latin crown", that is the upper part of the crown, consists of four arched gold bands, broken in several places. At their meeting-point on the top of the crown there is a square field, which also represents the enthroned Christ. The lower ends of the bands were attached to the upper part of the "Greek crown". On both sides of Christ there is a cypress, with the sun and the moon depicted in a circular field above them. The eight plates on the four bands were made with a different technique from that of the enamel plates on the lower band. They show eight apostles with their Latin names. St Bartholomew on the front band is covered by the picture of Christ, which is situated higher. Above him, also on the front band, is St John; the left-side band shows St Andrew, and above him St Peter, the right-side band depicts St Philip and above him St Paul, while on the back there is St Thomas, covered by the representation of Michael Ducas, placed higher, and above him, St James. Since only eight of the twelve apostles are represented here, it seems an obvious conclusion that the bands originally were not made for the crown.

The image of Christ on the top of the crown was pierced with a hole to hold a small gold cross, which is now in a slanting position.

13 (a) Sceptre

The rock-crystal head presumably dates from the 10th century, while the setting with filigree ornamentation is in all probability linked with the reign of King Béla III. Length: 37.5 cm; diameter of head: 7 cm

The wooden handle is covered with silver-gilt filigree work (now broken), the head of a rock-crystal ball is in a gold filigree setting. The side of the crystal ball is decorated with three lions, presumably of Egyptian work. The gold setting consists of flower cups, connected with three gold bands. The filigree decoration is composed of a row of palmettes divided by heart-shaped leaves. On top of the ball is a magic knot, known as having been considered potent against malign powers. Small balls hang on thin chains from the bands and flower cups.

13 (b) Orb

It was made presumably to replace the original orb of the Hungarian kings early in the 14th century. Height: 16.2 cm

A gilded copper sphere assembled from two halves, surmounted by a double cross. On the side of the body there is an enamelled coat of arms with red and white stripes of the Arpadian, and with the fleur-de-lis of the Angevin kings.

14 Sword

It was made in the 16th century, presumably in Venice, to replace the former royal sword that had disappeared. Length: 97.3 cm; width of cross-bar: 17 cm

The blade is double-edged, with Renaissance decoration at the hilt. The cross-bar is bent, the hilt ends in a knob. The sheath is made of wood and is covered with velvet.

15 Coronation Mantle

According to its inscription the mantle was made in 1031 for the Church of Our Lady at Székesfehérvár. Length (spread out): 132 cm; width: 262 cm

Originally a closed chasuble, it was later recut and decorated with a collar, presumably under the reign of King Béla III. It is of green silk decorated with lilac-red rosettes, but the colours have faded. The figures are embroidered in gold and silk thread. The figure of Christ in the centre is flanked by that of the Virgin to His right and St John the Baptist to the left. In the field above the inscription are the figures of prophets, and below it, six apostles flank the enthroned Christ on each side. The bottom stripe is embroidered with figures of martyrs in circular medallions. In the middle the two historical persons are King Stephen, holding a spear and the orb, with Queen Gisela at his side. Next to both figures their names are marked in Latin. Between them is a young child, presumably Prince Emeric. According to tradition the mantle was made in the nunnery at Veszprémvölgy.

16 Aquamanile

Beginning of 13th century. Found during railway construction work.
From between Abaújszentandrás and Abaújszántó.
Height: 42.5 cm (defective)

The object is made of copper. The upper part is a human figure ending in a horse body. The legs and tail of the centaur were cast separately and soldered to the body. The human head wears long hair, a short full-beard and moustache. The back of the head, which was formed out of the hinged lid, is missing. The figure holds in his left hand a drum with pierced holes and raises his right hand to strike a blow. A dragon-headed spout projects from the edge of the drum, which served as the pouring lip. The body of the horse is covered with punched decoration of circles and dots. The centaur carries a child playing a flute on his back. The garments of the human figure and the child are formed out of an incised design of ribbons and lines, with their belts decorated with parallel incised lines.

17 Head Reliquary

Height: 37.7 cm; breast: 53.5 cm
Provenance: Trencsén (now Trenčín, Czechoslovakia)

An outstanding example of fourteenth-century Hungarian goldsmith's art. The herm presumably depicts the canonized King Ladislas and was made of gilded copper with *repoussé* technique. The opening on the top of the skull served to hold the case of the relic. It was originally covered by a head-dress or a crown. The face is decorated with curly moustache and short, parted beard, the shoulders are covered by loose, soft drapes ending in a round, upright neck. The front of the cloth is decorated with punched scroll-work. At the bottom the reliquary ends in a wavy, fluted border. The nails and holes on the breast and around the shoulders suggest that the garment might have been ornamented with precious stones, these however have been lost.

18 Bone Saddle (detail)

End of 14th century–early 15th century
Height: 37 cm; width: 45 cm; length: 56 cm

The saddle consists of flat, embossed, ornate bone plates, which were earlier considered to be ivory, with the ribbon-like border made of antlers. The carving seems to indicate that it was not used for riding, rather for carrying valuables and weapons on ceremonial processions. Out of the two dozen bone saddles known internationally three are in the National Museum. Their provenance is not fully clarified, but it is certain that most of them were manufactured during the reign of Sigismund of Luxembourg, who from 1387 to his death in 1437 was king of Hungary and between 1411 and 1437 Holy Roman emperor as well. Research workers hold the view that Sigismund presented the saddles to the knights of the Order of the Dragon, which he himself founded in support of his rule. The motif of St George and the dragon often features on the saddles. The saddle in this picture shows the figures of St George the dragon-slayer and a kneeling princess, with lutenists, amorous couples, a unicorn, a man fighting a lion, dragons, stags and hounds. The tone and style of presentation are related to those of early fifteenth-century secular murals and tapestries. The Latin inscription on the left side of the pommel in a banderole reads: "DA PACEM DOMINE" (Give us peace, o Lord). On the cantle is the emblem of the Order of the Dragon. The saddles were possibly made in the workshops of King Sigismund's Buda court, and are works of Franco-Flemish or Italian master craftsmen.

19 Gothic Chalice
15th century. Height: 27.3 cm; diameter of mouth: 11.9 cm; diameter of foot: 15.7 cm
Provenance: the church at Torna.
Silver gilt. The figures of St Peter, St Paul, St Ladislas, St Emeric, St Stephen and St John the Baptist are incised on the six-lobed foot. The sixth segment has a silver plate attached to it, with the half-length portrait of a crowned princess in an escutcheon against a black enamelled background. St Barbara's half-length figure appears above the coat of arms of the Forgách family. The stem carries the inscription: "MARIA HILF" (Help us, Mary) in Gothic chapels, and the cup grows out of its top of the shape of a truncated pyramid. The figures of saints incised on the cup, showing traces of green enamelling, are the Virgin Mary with the Child, St Margaret, St Peter, St Paul, St Barbara and St Elizabeth. The inscription in Gothic minuscules in a punched belt running round the cup reads: "HIC EST CALIX NOVI TESTAMENTI IN MEO SANGVINE" (This is the chalice of the New Testament with my blood). The foot has the incised inscription: "CALICEM NUNC MUSAEO NATIONALI DONAVIT JOANNES COMES KEGLEVICH DE BUZIN S.C.R.A. MTATIS CAMERARIVS, 1815" (This chalice was given to the National Museum in 1815 by Count Johannes Keglevich, the chamberlain of His Holy Royal Imperial and Apostolic Highness).

20 Glass Goblet of King Matthias Corvinus
Second half of 15th century. Height: 43 cm; diameter of base: 23 cm; diameter of mouth: 27.5 cm
The funnel-shaped cup and the knob are of white striped glass. The foot had been broken and lost, and was replaced—presumably by copying the original form as faithfully as possible—by silver gilt, at the end of the sixteenth or the beginning of the seventeenth century. The legend on the foot in capital letters reads: "VINA BIBANT HOMINES ANIMALIA COETERA FONTES" (Men should drink wine, the other animals water). Also on the foot are 36 lines of a Hungarian rhymed inscription, telling the story of the goblet: King Matthias Corvinus had acquired it from the Venetians and used it for drinking toasts. Later it passed to King Louis II, who donated it to Ferenc Batthyány; in the late nineteenth century it came to the Erdődy family, who presented it to the National Museum in 1929. The goblet is an eminent piece of fifteenth-century Venetian (Murano) glass-work.

21 King Matthias Corvinus's Throne Tapestry
From the 1470s. Length: 252 cm; width: 160–161 cm

The gold brocade is woven of yellow and green silk threads and on the obverse fully brocaded in gold. In the upper third of the tapestry is the quartered coat of King Matthias Corvinus in a wreath of oak leaves, with the coat of arms of Hungary in the upper two quarters and those of Dalmatia and Bohemia in the two lower ones. In the centre the heart-shaped escutcheon displays the family arms of the Hunyadis: a raven holding a ring in its beak. The design for the throne tapestry was presumably made by Antonio Pollaiuolo, and the tapestry itself was produced in a Florentine workshop, commissioned by the king. It is an outstanding specimen of Renaissance art.

22 Ornamental Papal Sword of King Wladislas II

1509. Lengths: blade: 106.8 cm; sheath: 112.4 cm; belt: 227 cm

The large, straight, double-edged blade has the figures of St Peter and St Paul on its two sides, up at the hilt. It bears the inscription:

"IULIUS II PONT. MAX. ANNO. VII.", and is decorated with a flowery branch as well as the pope's coat of arms with the oak-tree of the della Rovere family in a dentate circle. The papal tiara appears above the shield; all the engravings are gilded. The hilt has a treble division, a silver-gilt cross-bar, and terminates in a big, silver-gilt pommel with a rich ornamentation of acanthus leaves. There is a laurel wreath in the middle which once surrounded the della Rovere coat of arms. The wooden sheath is covered with red fabric and holds an openwork silver-gilt plate with artistic enamel decoration. The oblong enamel plaque at the end of the sheath bears the papal coat of arms. The gold brocade sword-belt is decorated with the della Rovere arms, the papal tiara, St Peter with the key and oak foliage.

The papal sword was the work of Domenico di Michele de Sutri, the goldsmith of Pope Julius II, and was a present from the pope to King Wladislas II, as the leader of the struggle against the Turks.

23 Ornamental Weapons

(a) Pointed Dagger. 16th century.
Length: 135 cm; width of blade: 2.3 cm
Four-edged Turkish blade with an S-shaped cross-bar. The hilt terminates in a pear-shaped pommel made of wire. The silver-gilt sheath is surrounded with five thin cross-bands (one missing), which hold lobed, broadening plaques attached to the obverse, with turquoise-girded nephrite-plates in their middle; the sheath is decorated with these plates in other places too. The reticular pattern on the reverse of the sheath flanks scrollornamented fields.

(b) Sabre. First half of 17th century.
Length: 97 cm; width of blade: 3.5 cm.
It belonged to János Kemény, Prince of Transylvania.

The oriental scroll design on the Genoese blade is inlaid with silver and gold at the hilt. The hilt itself is lapped round with silver-gilt wire, and terminates in a low pommel. The sheath is covered with red velvet and complete with three almond-shaped rosette bands. The bands, the middle of the cross-bar and the top of the pommel are richly ornamented with Transylvanian *cloisonné* enamel and turquoises.

24 Pálffy Goblet with Cover

Height: 42.8 cm; height of cup: 25.4 cm; diameter of mouth: 13.4 cm; diameter of base: 10.6 cm

Miklós Pálffy received the splendid gold goblet with coloured enamelling as a present from the Estates of Lower Austria after the recapture of the town of Győr in 1598.

The base is circular, the vase-shaped stem has a twofold division which holds the double-arched, hemispherical cup, and terminates in a broad, smooth rim. The rim of the base is decorated in white enamel, and the ornament above it consists of a design resembling an ear, war insignia and musical instruments. The lower part of the goblet represents various trophies, and the upper part has eight groups of ornaments, two each being diagonally identical: (a) the coat of arms of Lower Austria; (b) trophies with a red and white flag and the flag with the imperial black eagle; (c) a winged mask; (d) trophies with a white Turkish flag with the crescent and a star. Of the eight ornate fields on the cover two again show the coat of arms of Lower Austria, two include trophies, and four represent cartouches with shell decoration. The place of the knob is taken by the figure of a Roman warrior in ornate helmet, with war trophies under his feet. His left foot rests on a severed Turkish head. The oval shield on his back is decorated with the imperial coat of arms with the double-eagle. On the sides are the Hungarian coat of arms with an apostolic cross, the heraldic lion of the Bohemian coat of arms, and the Austrian arms with a red slanting fesse. The shield is framed by the inscription, "GOT DIE ER. 1598", in black enamelled letters.

25 RUDOLF ALT (Vienna 1812–Vienna 1905):
View of the Hungarian National Museum
Colour lithograph by Franz Xaver Sandmann after a drawing by R. Alt. Size: 19.4 × 26.1 cm
Rudolf Alt, (1812–1905) member of an Austrian family of painters, was himself a landscape artist. During his visits to Hungary he made drawings of numerous buildings.

Museum of Fine Arts

Both in terms of the importance of the material and the quantity of objects it contains, the Museum of Fine Arts in Budapest holds an outstanding place among the country's museums with a similar range of contents. The institution collects works of European art ranging from the great ancient Mediterranean cultures to contemporary paintings, sculpture and graphic art.

The establishment of the Museum was decided on during the millenary celebrations marking the 1000th anniversary of the Hungarian Conquest of the country. Its foundation was established in the Millenary Act of 1896, and the Museum was opened in December 1906.

But the origin of the collection reaches back even farther. The material in the Hungarian National Museum, which was founded by Count Ferenc Széchényi in 1802, included, together with its collection of books, coins and antiquities, a few paintings, mainly historical portraits. After the pictures had been arranged, an exhibition was mounted in the Museum under the name of Hungarian National Gallery. The material consisted of pictures donated by the founder, Ferenc Széchényi, and later purchases, such as paintings from the collection of the historian Miklós Jankovich, purchased in the 1830s, as well as some major gifts, for example the 190 pieces presented by János László Pyrker, Archbishop of Eger, and the bequest of Bishop Arnold Ipolyi of Besztercebánya (now Banská Bystrica, Czechoslovakia). After the completion of the museum building at Hősök tere (Heroes' Square), the paintings and engravings in the National Museum were classified and divided, and amalgamated with the collections of the Esterházy Gallery, which was temporarily housed in the Hungarian Academy of Sciences. That became the contents of the Gallery of Old Masters and the Department of Drawings and Prints which together formed the backbone of the Museum of Fine Arts. The first objects in the collections of old Hungarian works, old sculptures and "modern" foreign pieces also came from the relevant collection of the National Museum. The Collection of Old Hungarian Masters has meanwhile been transferred to the Hungarian National Gallery.

DEPARTMENT OF EGYPTIAN ART. Up till the end of the last century, the collection of ancient Egyptian works also formed part of the Department of Antiquities of the Hungarian National Museum. The excavations carried out near Sharuna and Gamhoud in Central Egypt at the beginning of the century, which were financed in part by the Hungarian Fülöp Back, resulted in a considerable increase in the quality and quantity of the collection. The Hungarian, Austrian and Polish teams participating in the excavations were given wooden coffins and grave goods dating from Ptolemaic and Roman times, as well as some splendid Ptolemaic relief wall fragments. Other Egyptian material dispersed in various museums in the country were later united in the Department of Antiquities of the Museum of Fine Arts. That was the time for a systematic, scholarly arrangement of the material, and as a result the first collective exhibition of Egyptian art was opened in 1939. The war caused grave damage to the collection, but after the country's liberation in 1945, the collection was enlarged by further important pieces, the most notable of them having come from the bequest of Abbot Bonifác Platz of Zirc. In 1957, the Egyptian collection was separated from the Department of Antiquities, and in 1962 was made into an independent department that offers a varied picture on the various periods and genres of ancient Egyptian culture, its death cult and art. In 1959, some relics were bought from Egypt which have filled a gap. In 1964, following a Unesco appeal, a Hungarian expedition took part in the partial excavation of a town and graveyard in Abdallah Nirqi, north of Abu Simbel in Upper Nubia. The Egyptian authorities placed a major part of the finds at the disposal of the Hungarian expedition, and that material (some 2,500 pieces) now also enriches the Egyptian collection.

DEPARTMENT OF ANTIQUITIES. The idea of setting up a collection of original antique pieces did not emerge at the foundation of the Museum of Fine Arts. They had plaster casts of the classical masterpieces made and displayed them in the ground-floor halls of the Museum. But in 1908, on the recommendation of Antal Hekler, the Museum purchased 135 marble statues from the Munich archaelogist Paul Arndt. This collection, together with the 650 pieces of terracotta acquired from Arndt in 1913, formed the foundations of the collection of antiquities. The basis of the collection of vases was a gift from Marcell Nemes in 1917. When in 1935, the section became an independent department, it already possessed a considerable collection. The years after the country's liberation brought further additions and expansion. The rearrangement of the contents of the provincial museums resulted in a number of pieces coming to Budapest; the Haán collection from the museum in Gyula was particularly valuable. The cylix of the Andocides Painter, a piece of international importance, came to the Museum from that collection. Major purchases have included the collection of gems bought from Rousopoulos Rhoussos in Greece, the antiquities Count Ferenc Zichy collected in Cyprus, and the Corinthian vases the engineer Pál Gerster acquired during his work at the construction of the Corinth Canal.

The Department preserves outstanding pieces from the Greek, Etruscan, Roman and Carthaginian cultures. Among the relics of Bronze Age cultures in what subsequently became Greek territory, two marble female figures from the third millennium B.C. and the Bronze Age pottery from Cyprus are of major importance. The Greek material is proud to contain original marble statues, in particular the archaic torso of a youth, masterpieces of Athenian grave sculptures from the fourth century B.C. and the early Hellenistic figure of a girl known as the "Budapest Dancer". In the rich collection of terracotta all the major workshops of the archaic, classical and Hellenistic ages are represented; particularly rich is the material from the Boeotian archaic and classical periods, the Greek clay statuettes from Southern Italy from the fifth to fourth centuries B.C., the so-called Tanagra figurines from the fourth to third centuries B.C., as well as the Hellenistic grotesque statuettes and the series of Egyptian terracotta from the Roman age. The Department of Antiquities boasts of two major works of Greek bronze-casting, an archaic jug and the "Grimani jug" of remarkable beauty from the mid-fifth century B.C. The collection of bronze weapons includes an example of each of the Greek helmet types of the archaic period. The art of Greek goldsmithing is represented mainly by fourth to second-century jewels, as well as a gold diadem from the eighth century B.C.

The outstanding collection of Greek vases is arranged around several historical and technical turning-points, such as the rich collection of vessels from Cyprus, the Corinthian vases from the seventh and sixth centuries B.C., masterpieces of Athenian black and red-figure vases from the sixth and fifth centuries, including works by such eminent masters as the amphora by Exekias, an archaic Greek vase painter of the highest artistic ability, a cup by the Andocides Painter, the founder of red-figure vase painting, and a late work of the Brygos Painter. Notable pieces represent the Greek red-figure vase painting of Southern Italy from the fourth century B.C. as well.

Of the archaic material of Etruscan art mention should be made of the series of terracotta antefixes from Campania used for the decoration of buildings, black-figure vases and bronze pieces, as well as a few large-size terracotta heads of gods.

The backbone of the Roman material consists of marble sculptures, including a series of Roman portrait sculpture ranging from the first century B.C. to the third century A.D., some world-famous pieces of Roman reliefs (e.g. the Lecce relief from the second century B.C. and the so-called Actium relief from the time of Augustus, and a sarcophagus depicting a hunting scene, originating from an Athenian workshop in the third century B.C.), and interesting votive and grave statues from Roman occupied territories, which illustrate the incipient approach of the Middle Ages.

Carthaginian culture is represented by pottery and a few rare relics of clay sculpture in the collection of some 4,000 objects.

GALLERY OF OLD MASTERS. This forms the heart of the contents of the Museum, and contains the most remarkable collection, which is widely known beyond the country's borders. Of the nearly 2,700 paintings by old foreign masters about 800 are displayed in a permanent exhibition, with the rest on show in the rooms of a study collection arranged as a gallery and open to professionals. These paintings are of high artistic merit, and are also used to replace the pieces in the permanent exhibition which are occasionally lent for temporary exhibitions or other major displays both in Hungary and abroad.

A whole range of collections, acquired by the Museum through purchases, presents and bequests have played a major role in developing the present aspect of the Gallery. The exclusively historical paintings and engravings of the collection of the Széchényi General Gallery were enlarged with the purchase of the Jankovich collection around 1832, which included some works of art of historical significance. By a happy chance, the collection included some interesting pieces by fifteenth and sixteenth-century Austrian and German painters, which at that time were still held in small esteem and scarcely collected—predominantly altar-pieces. Together with some sixteenth-century pictures from Venice and Upper Italy, it was from that collection that the Museum acquired its first Spanish painting, an allegorical depiction called *Human Passions* by the Alcira Master from the vicinity of Valencia, painted in the mid-sixteenth century. In 1836, János László Pyrker, Archbishop of Eger, formerly Bishop of Szepes, and later Patriarch of Venice, presented a valuable collection to the National Museum, consisting mostly of Italian pictures. The prelate was of Hungarian birth, but active in the Austrian literary scene, and he was prouder of his epic poems written in German and extolling various members of the Habsburg House than of his activity as a collector, although the paintings he purchased from Venetian collections, art dealers and restorers included a number of works which contributed to founding the fame of the Museum, as for example Gentile Bellini's half-length *Portrait of Caterina Cornaro, Queen of Cyprus,* Giorgione's splendid *Portrait of a Youth,* and the fragment of a contemporary copy of his picture depicting *The Finding of Paris,* which had been lost, paintings from the schools of Titian, Tintoretto and Veronese, Vincenzo Catena's typical, signed panel *The Holy Family with a Holy Woman,* some rare German and Netherlandish paintings, such as Jacob Grimmer's panels depicting the seasons and Hans Memling's splendid *Baptism of Christ,* which the prelate acquired with a forged Cranach signature from Baron Imre Vay in the village of Kékcse, Szabolcs County, during one of his canonical visitations in the second quarter of the last century. Examples by sixteenth to eighteenth-century Venetian painters include canvases from Palma Vecchio, Lorenzo Lotto and several *vedute* showing the environs of Venice by Francesco Guardi and his son Giacomo, as well as works by Bernardo Bellotto and Marieschi and Giovanni Battista Tiepolo's delightful *The Virgin with Six Saints;* these all came to the Museum from the Pyrker collection. Augustin Quesnel's panel *Woman Playing the Guitar* is a signed and dated work by a master whose works are rarely found, and the collection also included some works by German, French and Hungarian painters who can be considered contemporaries of the archbishop, and the best pieces of which are displayed in the Museum's permanent exhibition.

The extremely rich Italian material in the Pyrker collection and the subsequent Ipolyi bequest still form the representative core of fourteenth to sixteenth-century Italian art in the Gallery.

Canon Arnold Ipolyi, the director of the Pest seminary, was well known for his historical research work. Author of the volume *Magyar mitológia* (Hungarian Mythology) and later chairman of the Society of Fine Arts, Ipolyi became Bishop of Besztercebánya in 1872, and presented part of his collection, primarily fourteenth-century Italian paintings, to the National Gallery. The works were to supplement the material of the Esterházy Gallery, which was purchased nearly at the same time. They include one of the panels of Spinello Aretino's *chef-d'œuvre,* the triptych originally made for the monastic church of Sta Maria Nuova in Rome and erected only later in the Monteoliveto abbey near Siena; and a beautiful *Madonna* by Ambrogio Lorenzetti. The events of the 1848 Revolution enlarged the Hungarian National Museum's General Gallery with 75 paintings from the Imperial Court Collections in Vienna, as the country's governor, Lajos Kossuth, called upon the director of the National Museum to have the oil paintings at the residence of the chairman of the Buda Treasury examined, "as those to be selected from them will be conveyed to the museum". The paintings came from Vienna to the castle of Pozsony (now Bratislava, Czechoslovakia) in 1770, when the Empress Maria Theresa had the vice-regent's residence refurnished on the occasion of the marriage between Archduchess Maria Christina and Prince Albert of Saxony. The paintings include a number of valuable works: Albrecht Dürer's *Portrait of a Man,* Lorenzo Lotto's canvas, *The Sleeping Apollo and the Dispersing Muses,* Palma Vecchio's enchanting portrait of a girl, whose complementary piece, the *Portrait of a Youth,* also formed part of the Court collections and was presented to the Museum in 1907.

The first independent exhibition opened in the National Museum in 1851, in the rooms called the Pyrker Gallery.

But the most important source of the material of the Museum of Fine Arts was the National Gallery housed in the Academy of Sciences, the core of which consisted of the collection of the Esterházy Gallery, purchased by the state in 1870. Originally the Esterházy Gallery was one of the sights of the imperial city of Vienna. When in 1815 the prince purchased the Kaunitz palace in Mariahilferstrasse, which at the time was still considered a suburb, the rooms equipped for his collection were open to the public on certain days of the week. Most of the foreigners visiting Vienna went to see the gallery which abounded in masterpieces, and many itineraries and reports describe the splendid paintings which represented practically all aspects of the European schools. From the mid-nineteenth century on, Hungarian newspapers and journals repeatedly gave voice to the public request that the "Prince Esterházy Gallery should be replanted from among the walls of Vienna to the bosom of the Hungarian fatherland which had provided the means for the illustrious princely family to collect such major art treasures".

In 1865, Prince Pál Esterházy yielded to the widely voiced request. Special rooms were set up for the collection in the building of the Hungarian Academy of Sciences, which was being built at the time, and soon the Hungarian public could marvel at the masterpieces. Since the Gallery was moved to Pest, not only the world-famous Esterházy collection of Italian, Netherlandish and Spanish masters, unmatched in Europe at the time except in Spain, could be put on display. In 1875 the collection was further expanded by some hundred canvases from among the most beautiful paintings of old masters transferred from the National Museum's Gallery to the Academy in order to exhibit them jointly in the National Gallery. Of the Italian masterpieces of the Esterházy collection, special mention should be made of the *Virgin and Child* signed by the Venetian Carlo Crivelli from the end of the fifteenth century; the poetically inspired panel *Virgin and Child with an Angel* by Correggio of Parma, which Prince Miklós Esterházy had purchased from Cardinal Crivelli; Boltraffio's *Madonna,* reflecting the influence of Leonardo da Vinci, and Raphael's masterpiece known as the *Esterházy Madonna.* Ridolfo Ghirlandaio's work, *The Adoration of the*

Shepherds, dating from 1510, also comes from the Esterházy collection, as do Tintoretto's early work *The Supper at Emmaus* and Giovanni Battista Tiepolo's large-size altar-piece which he made for the Spanish ambassador to London. Of the northern schools, Rembrandt's *Old Rabbi,* Frans Hals's expressive self-portrait, and the masterful portrait of a woman attributed to Vermeer van Delft are of outstanding importance. Of the Flemish painters, the pictures by Jordaens, and the joint work of Sir Anthony van Dyck and Rubens, *Mucius Scaevola before Porsenna,* are representative Baroque compositions. Seventeenth-century Netherlandish landscape painting is represented by works by Jan van Goyen, Jan Asselyn, Jacob van Ruisdael and his uncle Salomon van Ruysdael. The collection also included still lifes and genre pieces by notable Dutch and Flemish masters.

The bulk of the justly famous Spanish collection was purchased for Prince Miklós Esterházy by his son Pál from Count Edmund Burke in London between 1818 and 1821. Several fine pieces, including Ribera's *The Martyrdom of St Andrew,* and two captivating pieces of genre-painting from Goya, reached the Esterházy collection through purchases from the Vienna Kaunitz collection, as did works by great Baroque masters (Cano, Zurbarán, Cerezo, Murillo, Coello and Escalante) and the panel *Christ with the Eucharist* by the sixteenth-century master Juan de Juanes. The 637 items of the Esterházy Gallery also included some noted French pictures (Claude Lorrain: *Villa in the Roman Campagna,* Simon Vouet: *Apollo and the Muses*) and some English paintings.

The material, which could justly be ranked among the best European museums, was further expanded with outstanding works acquired by the Gallery's first learned director, Károly Pulszky. He purchased mural paintings and rare panels with great care and expertise during his travels abroad, making the best use of the 500,000 forints allocated by the state to the National Gallery in preparation for the festivities to be organized on the 1000th anniversary of the Hungarian Conquest in 896. Pulszky acquired a large-size altar-piece by Giovanni dal Ponte, a *Madonna* by Filippino Lippi, and an altar panel by the Umbrian Giovanni Boccati painted is a slightly archaic style in 1473. His purchases abroad also enlarged the Museum with a specific, unique collection: he searched for murals in Italian palaces and churches which were due to be demolished or rebuilt, and thus laid the foundations for the famous collection of frescoes displayed in the ground-floor corridors and the Renaissance hall of the Museum.

Of the late medieval material of the northern schools, Pulszky acquired an extremely delicate picture by Gerard David, *The Nativity,* and Barend van Orley's portrait of the young Emperor Charles V. He enriched the seventeenth-century Dutch collection, among other pieces, with a Rembrandt, *The Dream of St Joseph,* and a composition by Rembrandt's pupil Aert de Gelder, *Esther and Mordecai.*

The untimely tragic death of Pulszky slowed down the rate of purchases, but did not put an end to them. Under the directorship of Gábor Térey, the collection was enlarged with three panels by Hans Baldung Grien, the characteristic *Village Wedding Procession* by Jan Lys of Oldenburg and the remarkable canvas by Jan Kupezky, *Man Playing the Shawm.* The management of the Gallery kept an eye on auctions abroad and acquired a number of major works, for example, in 1904 from the Somzée collection in Brussels and in 1912 from the Weber collection in Hamburg.

The imposing palace built for the Museum of Fine Arts in Hősök tere, next to the City Park, was opened in 1906. Together with the other collections, the material of the Esterházy Gallery was also transferred to the new building. The management of the Gallery continued to keep track of offers which occurred to the art trade abroad and enriched the collection with a number of fine pieces. Meanwhile it also provided room for Marcell Nemes's pictures by foreign masters, which he exhibited temporarily in the Museum. Later this notable discriminating art-collector presented quite a few of these pictures to the Museum, while others have found their final home, after long peregrinations, in some of the great European and American collections. Of the purchases two Spanish paintings are of special interest: an early Velázquez canvas, bought from R. Langton Douglas in 1908, *Peasants at Table,* and an early work by Goya, the portrait of Manuela, the wife of the art writer, Ceán Bermúdez. The English School was originally represented only by a few works and was enriched at that time with a typical portrait each by Sir Henry Raeburn and William Hogarth, and Thomas Gainsborough's portrait of Charles Hotchkiss, as well as a small landscape depicting the *Waterloo Celebrations at East Bergholt* by John Constable. In 1912, the paintings in the Museum of Fine Arts were enriched with another bequest: the Italian and Netherlandish works of Count János Pálffy's gallery from his palaces in Vienna, Bazin (now Pezinok, Czechoslovakia), Pozsony and Budapest. The 177 pieces of old masters and a large number of nineteenth-century works include portraits by Titian, Paolo Veronese, a large-size altar-piece by Boltraffio, landscapes by Salomon van Ruysdael and Jan van Goyen, and notable pieces by Jan Steen, Gerbrandt van den Eeckhout and Bartholomeus van der Helst. With shrinking state subsidies, private donations came to the fore, particularly from collectors from the upper middle classes. Marcell Nemes enriched the Gallery of Old Masters especially with Spanish pictures, including five panels of a dismounted retable by the "Budapest Master" and El Greco's enchanting *Mary Magdalene;* while with Jan Kupezky's self-portrait with his family, he enriched the Museum's permanent exhibition with one of the principal works of the painter born in Hungary. The efforts of Elek Petrovics, the director-general of the Museum of the day, led to the donation of major works by other collectors too, such as Frigyes Glück and his fellow art patrons, as well as the Hungarian-born American Colonel Jenő Boross, who presented fine Spanish and Italian paintings to the country (Juan Carreño de Miranda: *St James the Greater Conquers the Moors;* Jacopo Bassano: *Christ Carrying the Cross* and Luis Tristán: *The Adoration of the Magi*).

The years between the two world wars saw a slackening in the expansion of the collection. A major event at this period was the Venice Convention of 1932, according to which certain paintings from the Imperial Court Collections of Vienna came to Hungary, including the two side panels of Hans Memling's triptych (the central piece having been presented to the National Museum a hundred years earlier by Pyrker), a Tintoretto and the *Portrait of the Infanta Margarita Theresa* painted in the workshop of Velázquez.

In the closing stages of the Second World War, the most famous pieces of the collection were taken to the West. The valuable collections were dispatched without adequate preparation, listing or wrappings. It is a real wonder that amidst the bombardments and fighting 95 paintings were returned from Szentgotthárd on the western border of the country with only relatively minor damage in 1945, with another 322 valuable works regained from Bavaria in 1946. The losses were insignificant and mostly due to the lack of control during transportation. Since then some additional smaller pictures have also turned up, for example valuable small pictures by J. A. Wtewael, Jan Brueghel the Elder and Francesco Guardi, which have been retrieved from the art trade in Hungary, and a remarkable work of Hans von Aachen from abroad.

The new acquisitions of the years after the country's liberation began with a splendid study of a head by El Greco in 1945, followed by several purchases and the amalgamation of major collections of foreign paintings in the course of the rearrangement of the material in public collections. First among these in the 1950s was the acquisition of relevant material from the former György Ráth Museum, including outstanding pieces such as Rembrandt's *The Slaughtered Ox* and Sebastiano del Piombo's *Portrait of a Woman.* But that was surpassed both in number and quality by the Count Jenő Zichy bequest, which came to the Museum from the municipal collection and which had earlier been exhibited in the Municipal Gallery in the former Károlyi mansion. Outstanding pieces in this collection are the triptych Taddeo di Bartolo painted in the last years of the fourteenth century, the *Portrait of a Man* by Giovanni Battista Moroni, a Fugger portrait attributed to Lorenzo Lotto and a number of major works of the Netherlandish schools.

When in 1956 the collection of Hungarian painting and sculpture was separated from the collection of old and modern paintings and sculptures from other countries, the rooms which were thus vacated allowed for a more extensive selection from the contents of the Gallery of Old Masters to be displayed to the public. The exhibition reflects the great abilities of director-general Andor Pigler.

During the last 25 years, the management of the Museum has been searching throughout the country for works by foreign old masters suitable for inclusion in the Museum. They have purchased many valuable items both from private individuals and at auctions in Budapest, including Nicolas Poussin's *Rest on the Flight into Egypt,* a large-size canvas by David Teniers the Younger: *Landscape with Palace,* three retable sections of panels of Spanish primitives, which so rarely come onto the market, three splendid sixteenth-century Italian works from the former Sándor Lederer collection (Sodoma: *Lucretia,* Puligo: *The Death of Cleopatra* and Girolamo da Treviso: *Mary Adoring Her Sleeping Child),* a canvas by the Guardi brothers, which once served as a church banner, and some remarkable works by F. A. Maulbertsch.

DEPARTMENT OF DRAWINGS AND PRINTS. Next to the Gallery of Old Masters, the collection of nearly 100,000 pieces of graphic work forms the most important section of the Museum both in quantity and the high artistic level of the drawings and prints. The collection of drawings includes representatives of all the major schools from the fifteenth to the twentieth century; particularly works of Italian, German and Netherlandish masters, and a smaller number by French and English artists. The bulk of the collections dates from the sixteenth to the nineteenth centuries, with a considerably smaller number of pieces from the fifteenth and the twentieth centuries. However, the twentieth-century material is enriched by many drawings and rare prints by artists of Hungarian origin, which have reached the collection as presents or purchases.

The greatest treasures in the collection of drawings are three Leonardo studies and eleven sheets by Rembrandt. Of the Italian Renaissance masters Raphael, Correggio, Veronese and Tintoretto are represented with several drawings. Most outstanding in the seventeenth-century material are works by Guercino, G. B. Castiglione, Guido Reni and Salvator Rosa, and in the eighteenth-century material, Giovanni Battista and Giovanni Domenico Tiepolo, Guardi, Diziani and Fontebasso. The early German collections are also extremely rich. In the section of eighteenth-century German and Austrian works the drawings by F. A. Maulbertsch, Kremser-Schmidt and Troger are the most important; and among the sixteenth-century Netherlandish masters, Pieter Bruegel the Elder, Abraham Bloemaert, Jacques de Geyn, Goltzius and Jan Brueghel the Elder feature with fine drawings. The high artistic level of the greatest seventeenth-century masters is hallmarked, besides masterpieces by Rembrandt, by drawings of Jacob van Ruisdael, Adriaen van Ostade, Cuyp, Van Dyck, Rubens and Jordaens. Seventeenth-century French drawing is represented by the art of its two most important masters, Claude Lorrain and Nicolas Poussin; the eighteenth-century material includes masterpieces by Watteau, Boucher and Fragonard.

The nineteenth and twentieth-century material also abounds in French works, and indeed in works by outstanding masters such as Daumier, Delacroix, Camille Corot, Millet, Courbet, Manet, Monet, Renoir, Pissarro, Sisley, Signac, Cézanne, Gauguin, Degas, Toulouse-Lautrec and Picasso; and among the sculptors, sketches by Rodin and Maillol. Several splendid drawings represent the great Dutch painter of the period, van Gogh. Austrian Biedermeier style appears in a number of masterly drawings by Jacob and Rudolf Alt, Amerling, Clarot, Ender, Kriehuber and Lieder, which are more than mere sketches, many of them being complete, independent works.

The most valuable and important part of the collection of drawings originated from the Esterházy collection. From the end of the eighteenth century onwards, Prince Miklós Esterházy amassed during three decades, together with paintings, a rich collection of drawings and prints. He purchased three large private collections which went a long way to enrich his own material, and consequently the Museum's collections, with remarkable

24

masterpieces. The purchase of the Praun collection in 1801 added mainly sixteenth-century German and Italian drawings to the Esterházy collection.

Two years later the prince purchased the Franz Anton Nowohratsky-Kolowrath collection of prints and drawings, which mainly enlarged the material of prints, and also brought a few valuable drawings including four splendid pieces by Rembrandt.

The number of drawings was extensively enlarged in 1811 with the purchase of A. C. Poggi's Paris collection, which had Italian drawings as its core, but also included valuable pieces by seventeenth-century French and Netherlandish masters. Poggi had acquired these works of the great masters from the material in seventeenth and eighteenth-century private collections at auctions in Paris and London. The bulk of his drawings originated from the collections of Lely, Reynolds, Barnard, Richardson, Crozat, Mariette and Lempereur.

Besides acquiring major private collections, Miklós Esterházy was a regular customer of well-known art dealers and auctions. So in a relatively short time he developed a varied collection of drawings and prints, with major works representing every period and every school. The prince was aided in his purchases by the Viennese draughtsman and engraver Joseph Fischer, who later became the director of the prince's collections and who, as can be seen from many of his letters to the prince, followed offers which came up in the Viennese art trade with keen attention, and made his selection with great skill and good taste. The Esterházy family's collection of drawings and prints passed into the possession of the Hungarian state in 1870, together with their gallery, and consisted of 3,535 drawings and 51,301 prints.

After the foundation of the Museum of Fine Arts, in 1910, the Department of Drawings and Prints was enlarged by the rich bequest of the Hungarian painter István Delhaes, which consisted of 2,683 drawings and 14,454 engravings. The core of the Delhaes collection consisted of works by eighteenth and nineteenth-century masters, and so it served as an excellent supplement to the contents of the Esterházy collection, in which those two centuries were relatively poorly represented. Delhaes lived in Vienna, where he could purchase mainly Austrian and German works. The art school which developed around the Emperor Rudolph II about 1600, is amply represented in the collection of drawings. A whole range of eighteenth-century Austrian and Venetian drawings are also the result of Delhaes's enthusiasm for collecting.

A further major event in the history of the Department occurred in 1935, when Pál Majovszky left his splendid collection of modern drawings to the Museum of Fine Arts. Majovszky began collecting in 1911, with great foresight and the special aim of donating his collection to the Museum. He endeavoured to set up a collection that would trace the development of European drawing from the late eighteenth century up to the twentieth century. His collection centred on French masters from Ingres to Picasso. Of the English masters the eighteenth century is represented at the highest level with works by Hogarth, Rowlandson and Gainsborough; German masters are represented by Leibl, Liebermann and Slevogt, and Dutch drawing by van Gogh and Jongkind.

Besides the incorporation of the material from these major sources, the enlargement of the collection of drawings was ensured by regular purchases, the most substantial ones having taken place in the 1910s, a decade that saw the acquisition of several hundreds of valuable, primarily seventeenth-century Netherlandish and eighteenth to nineteenth-century French and German drawings. Donations of private individuals also enriched the Department, with the largest item being the Béla Procopius collection of several hundred pieces of seventeenth to nineteenth-century portrait miniatures.

The collection of prints is even more complete and well-balanced than that of the drawings, as the acquisition of graphic works of which many copies were made, constituted an easier task. A great part of the prints also came from the Esterházy collection, mainly sixteenth to eighteenth-century works. The Esterházy collection acquired the first edition of Goya's prints during the master's lifetime. The prints in the Delhaes collection included mainly nineteenth-century pieces. The prevailing management of the Museum has enlarged the materials from those two great private collections by regular purchase. For example, the acquisition of an early Picasso etching, a dry-point, is linked to the name of Elek Petrovics. Apart from a number of minor purchases, the material of two major collections should be mentioned. The Museum purchased Professor Gyula Elischer's Rembrandt etchings in 1904, and in the same year it acquired the collection of Baron László Podmaniczky, consisting mainly of eighteenth-century prints, from his heirs.

As a result of such a regular collecting policy, the Department today possesses virtually the complete works of the greatest masters of graphic art: Dürer, Rembrandt, Goya, Daumier and Toulouse-Lautrec. Besides the work of the greatest masters, the art of Altdorfer, Lucas Cranach, Mantegna, Marcantonio Raimondi, Callot, G. B. Tiepolo and G. D. Tiepolo, Lucas van Leyden and Goltzius is also represented by complete series.

19TH AND 20TH-CENTURY MASTERS. While the Gallery of Old Masters and the Department of Drawings and Prints are examples of how donations and systematic purchases can supplement each other successfully, the material of the nineteenth and twentieth-century masters reflects the changing tastes of various periods, the interests of the donors, and the often retrograde effect of cultural policies between the two wars. Most of the state purchases were made at official exhibitions, selected and arranged according to the political and inter-state relations of the relevant period. The earliest pieces in the collection, mainly the Austrian Biedermeier pictures and pieces from fashionable painters of the end of the nineteenth century, were taken over from the National Museum's General Gallery, and others from the National Gallery. In the present century, director-general Elek Petrovics attempted to fill the gaps with a skilful hand. The purchases of Camille Corot's *Souvenir de Coubron* and of one of the prized pieces of the collection, Édouard Manet's *Lady with Fan*, are linked to his name. A Delacroix study also features among his acquisitions.

Unfortunately the contents of private collections, these natural sustainers of museums, have mostly been taken abroad and only few of them have reached the Museum. After a few works purchased from contemporary artists in the Pyrker collection, the bequest of Count János Pálffy included several nineteenth-century pictures, such as works by painters of the Barbizon School, canvases by Troyon and Daubigny, an orphanage scene by the Dutch Josef Israels and *The Triumphal Arch of Titus in Rome*, Franz von Lenbach's most important youthful work.

DEPARTMENT OF ANTIQUE SCULPTURE. The Department was set up as an independent unit in 1955, and includes the collection of works of European sculpture from the fourth to the eighteenth century. The rich material is the result of a systematic acquisition policy by the Museum. Its core is the Italian series purchased for the Museum, mostly by Károly Pulszky, in Italy at the end of the nineteenth century. It was complemented in 1914 by the purchase of the collection of bronze statues belonging to István Ferenczy, a pioneer of Hungarian Neo-Classical sculpture, which the artist collected in Rome in the first decades of the nineteenth century. During the directorship of Elek Petrovics, systematic purchases further enriched the collection, which was later supplemented with donations and pieces transferred from other Hungarian museums. After the Second World War, there were few new purchases, and only during recent years has there been the acquisition of some important pieces, including a *St Anne with the Virgin and Child* in a rare type of iconographic representation, a fourteenth-century Flemish *Madonna* and a unique collection of Venetian fountains, unique in the whole of Europe—as a worthy continuation of the initial steps.

The noteworthy Italian material of the Department includes typical pieces representing sculptural development in Northern and Central Italy, as well as works by some major masters of figurative sculpture. Chronologically the first among them is the world-famous frontal of the high altar from Salerno Cathedral. One part of the collection includes an eleventh-century ivory relief depicting the *Creation of Birds and Fish*, a thirteenth-century wooden crucifix from Spoleto and works by leading masters of the Tuscan Quattrocento (Michelozzo Michelozzi, Agostino di Duccio, Neroccio, Francesco di Giorgio, the Robbia workshop and Desiderio da Settignano). The statue of Christ, which once was the principal figure of a splendidly composed group on a tympanum, is the work of Andrea del Verrocchio, the greatest master of the late Tuscan Quattrocento. The two kneeling angels which originally formed part of it, were taken to America. Worth of special mention is the small mounted figure, which was undoubtedly made after sketches by Leonardo da Vinci, and according to the latest research is supposed to portray King Francis I of France.

French cathedral sculpture is represented by a thirteenth-century head of St James the Apostle, while outstanding among works in the "soft style" that prevailed at the end of the fourteenth century, is a beautiful stone *Madonna*, the work of an east German (Prague?) sculptor, a widely known and much appreciated prototype of the "beautiful Madonnas". A real treasure of Gothic transcendental presentation is the life-size oak statue of *Mary and St John the Evangelist*, which belonged to the fifteenth-century calvary of the church in Grosskönigsdorf near Cologne. The influence of Italian Mannerism on German sculpture is exemplified by a few delicate bronze statues in the collection. Austrian Baroque, which both geographically and in its influence was closest to Hungary, is represented by a number of works, including lead reliefs and statues by Georg Raphael Donner.

DEPARTMENT OF MODERN FOREIGN SCULPTURE. The collection includes works of sculpture ranging from the 1800s to the present day, and forms part of the Department of Modern Art. Earlier the collection was included among recent Hungarian and foreign sculpture, and then of the Department of Antique Sculpture. The earliest French sculpture in the relatively small collection is *Spring*, a lovely terracotta head by Jean Baptiste Carpeaux. Auguste Rodin, the most renowned sculptor of the end of the nineteenth century, is represented by six statues. His early work, a large-size bronze, *The Bronze Age*, is followed by his *Nereids*, originally planned for Victor Hugo's monument, also known as *The Dance of the Sirens*. His portraits include those of two of his fellow artists, J. P. Laurens and A. Falquière, and a white marble copy of *Eternal Spring* is an outstanding piece from his mature period.

French sculptural art after Rodin is represented by three small bronzes by Aristide Maillol, including his famous *Leda*, and a beautiful piece by Charles Despiau, the *Portrait of Mme Bruce*. An example of contemporary trends is a black-and-white marble spatial construction by the noted abstract sculptor André Bloc, the sculptor's present to the Museum. The mobiles by Hungarian-born Nicolas Schöffer and works by Amerigo Tot represent the latest sculptural endeavours.

Belgian art is introduced by statues of Paul Maurice Dubois, Thomas Vincotte, Paul de Vigne and Jules Lagae, as well as a number of works by Constantin Meunier, including *The Dockworker*, *The Pit Pony Driver* and *The Foundryman*. The next generation is represented by three works by Georges Minne, among them his noted statue, *Boy Holding a Shell*.

Marianna Haraszti-Takács

27

26 Man's Portrait

Limestone. Egypt, New Kingdom. 19th dynasty (c. 1200 B.C.). Height: 22 cm

Originally the head might have been part of a complete statue. It represents in the Theban style a typical nobleman of the Rameses period. The head is of a delicate shape, under a finely detailed wig, and the noble simplicity and the almost decadent refinement of the features were conceived in the spirit of the unofficial sculpture of the 19th dynasty.

27 Niobid

Terracotta. 2nd century B.C. Height: 67 cm

This piece of Italian terracotta statuary originates from Sta Maria Capua Vetere, and formed part of a sculptural group on the tympanum of a temple in Southern Italy, depicting the destruction of the seven sons and seven daughters of Niobe by Apollo and Artemis. The youth of the Budapest statue is trying to protect himself from the arrows of the gods by holding his robe in front of his face.

28 Athenian Stele

Marble. c. 330 B.C. Height: 168 cm

This gravestone with three figures is the concluding piece from a row of classical Greek grave reliefs; the nudity of the male figure conventional way of portraying a hero, and it marks out the dead from among the living, as it were. The woman opposite him places her left hand on the man's shoulder and clasps his hand with her right, which links her with the dead husband. Between the two principal figures stands a little servant boy. The pathos of the scene and the style resolving the strict classical forms make the dating probable.

29 GENTILE BELLINI

(b. c. 1429, Venice–d. 1507, Venice):

The Portrait of Caterina Cornaro, Queen of Cyprus. c. 1500

Oil on poplar, 63 × 49 cm

The inscription in the upper left corner, now illegible, gave the names of the painter and the subject of the painting. Gentile Bellini was a member of the famous Bellini family of Venice. Few of his works have survived, but these include some portraits. Among them this work from his maturity is of major importance. Caterina Cornaro wears the same dress as in the painting depicting the miracle of a relic of the Holy Cross in the Gallery of the Academy of Venice, in which Gentile Bellini represented her among her ladies. In 1489 the Queen renounced the island she inherited from her husband, King James II Lusignan of Cyprus, in favour of the Republic of Venice. The painting originating from Venice might have been one of the studies the painter made for the major figures for his great composition. It was presented to the National Museum in 1836 by János László Pyrker, Archbishop of Eger, who in 1822–1827 was Patriarch of Venice.

30 MICHELE PANNONIO

(or Michele Ongaro, painter of Hungarian extraction, active in Ferrara from 1415 on; died between 1459 and 1464):

Muse Thalia. 1450–60

Tempera and oil on poplar, 136.5 × 82 cm

The inscription on the base of the throne refers to the subject as the incarnation of fertility, and is also included in the contemporary "programme", proposals for painters on the decoration of the study of Belfiore Castle near Ferrara. The inscription is divided by one of Borso d'Este's badges: a row of piles used in the draining of marshes, and a pumpkin floating on a wave. The painting was presented to the National Museum by Arnold Ipolyi in 1880. It is thought to have been in the Sala del Sant' Uffizio, the council chamber of the inquisition, near the Church of S. Domenico's in Ferrara in the eighteenth century. Originally the panel was painted for the study of the Duke of Ferrara. Several panels with portrayals of muses and seasons from among the decorations of the study.

31 RAPHAEL
(b. 1483, Urbino–d. 1520, Rome):
The "Esterházy Madonna". c. 1508
Oil and tempera on poplar, 28.5 × 21.5 cm
A pen-and-ink sketch to this unfinished picture is in the collection of the Uffizi Gallery in Florence. It was owned in succession by Pope Clement XI, the wife of Emperor Charles III, Queen and Empress Elisabeth Christina, and the Vienna collection of Prince Kaunitz. By 1812 it already featured in the catalogue of the Esterházy collection. Since the beginning of the last century, this famous painting with its enchanting beauty has been known in art literature as the "Esterházy Madonna". It dates from the beginning of Raphael's Roman period, and shows the influence of Leonardo da Vinci's Madonna drawings. From the Esterházy collection.

32 GIOVANNI ANTONIO BOLTRAFFIO
(b. 1467, Milan–d. 1516, Milan):
Virgin and Child. Late 15th century.
Oil and tempera on poplar, 83 × 63.5 cm
The Milan master was a pupil of Leonardo da Vinci, and the picture featured in the Esterházy collection as the work of Leonardo. According to recent research, Leonardo made a contribution to the picture which was painted in the last years of the fifteenth century. The gesture of the Child seems to indicate that Boltraffio originally painted a plant in the flower vessel, and this might have been destroyed during a restoration. The painting clearly reflects the dreamy charm of Leonardo's Madonnas, the soft transition of colours and the sculptural figures. From the Esterházy collection, where it first featured in the catalogue for the year 1820.

33 GIORGIONE
(Giorgio da Castelfranco; b. 1478, presumably in Castelfranco–d. 1510, Venice):
Portrait of a Youth (Antonio Broccardo?). (No date)
Oil on canvas, 72.5 × 54 cm
The by now fragmentary inscription in the middle of the painting reads:
ANTONIVS . BROKARDVS MAR . . .

In the middle of the parapet is a treble head in a wreath of leaves, flanked by a black hat with the white letter V on the left and a black tablet on the right. The canvas makes use of the best traditions of the Venetian Renaissance school of portraiture, but the reputed model, the Venetian poet Antonio Broccardo, was still a child at the time of Giorgione's death, and died young, in 1531. So the name in the inscription must be erroneous, or else the picture is the work of an eminent pupil of Giorgione. A recent explanation interprets the inscription as referring to a jurist. From the Pyrker collection, donated to the Museum in 1836.

34 ALBRECHT DÜRER
(b. 1471, Nuremberg–d. 1528, Nuremberg):
Portrait of a Man (Endres Dürer)
Oil on pine, 43 × 29 cm
The sketch for the picture is preserved in the Albertina Collection in Vienna, and according to the inscription on it, the model is the painter's younger brother. The portrait uses few external elements, and only concentrates on the face with its lively eyes and irregular features modelled against a light red background, as an example of Dürer's art of intimate portrayal. In the seventeenth century the picture was in the Brussels collection of Archduke Leopold Wilhelm, from where it came to the Imperial Court Collection in Vienna as part of the vice-regent's collection, then in 1770 to the Pozsony Castle, and from there, to the residence of the chairman of the Buda treasury, and in 1848, upon Lajos Kossuth's order, to the National Museum.

35 BAREND VAN ORLEY (b. 1487 or 1488, Brussels–d. 1452, Brussels):
Portrait of Emperor Charles V.
Late 1510s
Oil on oak, 71.5 × 51.5 cm
The portrait occupies an eminent place among the portrayals of Charles V, and shows the young emperor in a splendid gown, with the Order of the Golden Fleece on his breast. The Museum purchased the picture from the Bourgeois brothers in Cologne in 1894; earlier it formed part of the Ollingworth-Magniac Collection in

London. In 1907 it was displayed at the Exposition de la Toison d'Or in Bruges.

36 PIETER BRUEGEL THE ELDER
(b. 1525, Brueghel–d. 1569, Brussels):
St John the Baptist Preaching. 1566
Oil on oak, 95 × 160.5 cm
The idea of the subject might have been prompted by the frequent appearances of itinerant preachers disseminating Calvinistic and Lutheran doctrines, or the tenets of Anabaptist sects. The composition depicts all the tiny details with striking authenticity, and the figure of the saint is almost lost in the background. The popularity of the picture is borne out by a very large number of copies, both contemporary and dating from the seventeenth century (in Antwerp, Basel, Bonn, Bruges, Dresden, Cracow, Milan, Munich, Schwerin, etc.), most of them produced in the family workshop. From the Batthyány castle at Nagycsákány; it first featured at an exhibition in Szombathely in 1912.

37 GIOVANNI BATTISTA TIEPOLO
(b. 1696, Venice–d. 1770, Madrid):
St James the Greater Conquers the Moors. 1767–69
Oil on canvas, 317 × 163 cm
This monumental, animated composition with its sparkling colour effects dates from the mature period of the painter, depicting a scene of the Battle of Clavijo when, according to legend, the Apostle St James the Greater rose from his grave to assist the Spanish army against the Moors, helping his compatriots to victory. From the Esterházy collection, which acquired it in 1821.

38 JAN VAN GOYEN
(b. 1596, Leiden–d. 1656, The Hague):
Seascape with Fishermen
Oil on oak, 36.1 × 32.3 cm
This small piece, outstanding among the seven Goyens in the Museum's collection, is one of the painter's real masterpieces. The minute care of the representation of the overcast sky against a low horizon and the light, hazy atmosphere, is typical of Goyen's artistic approach. From the bequest of Count János Pálffy, from his Pozsony (now Bratislava, Czechoslovakia) mansion, 1912.

30

39 JOHANNES VERMEER VAN DELFT (?)
(b. 1632, Delft–d. 1675, Delft):
Portrait of a Woman. 1655–60
Oil on canvas, 82 × 65 cm
This portrait is of excellent quality, with its limited colour range, and was formerly considered to be a Rembrandt. In 1888, A. Bredius attributed it to Vermeer. More recent opinion still differs about the authorship, but scholars agree that it must be the work of a major master, dating from between 1655 and 1660. From the Esterházy collection, where it featured as a Rembrandt.

40 EL GRECO
(b. 1541, Candia, Crete–d. 1614, Toledo):
Study of a Man (Self-portrait?). *c.* 1590
Oil on canvas, 50 × 43 cm
The brooding, introspective man in this small-size canvas can scarcely be the head of an apostle as it was formerly held to be on the basis of the conventional garment, nor is it probable that it is simply a study for some major composition. The attempt at individualization seems to confirm the view that the painter portrayed his own features under the pretext of a figure dressed in a garment resembling the cloak of the apostles. The picture was once in the collection of the Marqués de Vega Inclán, and early this century was owned by Marcell Nemes. The Museum purchased it from the Herzog collection in 1945.

41 FRANCISCO DE GOYA
(b. 1746, Fuendetodos–d. 1828, Bordeaux):
The Water-seller (La aguadora).
Before 1812
Oil on canvas, 68 × 50.5 cm
In 1812 this painting was in the possession of Goya's son, Javier Goya, and by 1820, it featured, together with four other Goya genre pictures, at the Kaunitz auction in Vienna, where its companion piece was purchased for the Esterházy collection. *The Water-seller* came to the Esterházy collection from an auction organized by the Artaria firm of art dealers. A preparatory drawing for the picture came up for sale in Paris in 1973, with the inscription: *lastima es que no te ocupas en otra cosa* (a pity you don't deal with something else).

42 DIEGO VELÁZQUEZ
(b. 1599, Seville–d. 1660, Madrid):
Peasants at Table (El almuerzo).
c. 1617–18
Oil on canvas, 96 × 112 cm
The most typical *bodegóns,* Spanish kitchen scenes, were made in Seville, Andalusia. Young Velázquez painted many pictures of the type. He is known to have worked from studies made from nature. His first surviving picture of the type, *Breakfast,* which is in Leningrad, is an earlier variant of the Budapest picture, of which a great many copies and variants are known. This picture is perhaps identical with the copy mentioned in Cádiz in 1795. It came up for sale in a London auction in 1908 from A. Sanderson's Edinburgh collection.

43 CLAUDE MONET
(b. 1840, Paris–d. 1926, Giverny):
Fishing Boats. 1886
Oil on canvas, 73 × 92.5 cm
A mature, typically Impressionist work, the manner of animated and fresh presentation indicates that it was painted at one sitting. The scene recalls Étretat, a favourite resort of the artist. Purchased from István Herzog in 1945.

44 ÉDOUARD MANET
(b. 1832, Paris–d. 1883, Paris):
Lady with Fan. 1864. Signed 'Manet' in the lower left corner.
Oil on canvas, 90 × 113 cm
This splendid canvas is one of the most prized pieces in the Department of Modern Art, portraying Jeanne Duval, Baudelaire's famous, ill-famed mistress. The enormous hooped skirt of the dark-faced, half-reclining woman, already faded at the time, almost fills the canvas; the lace curtain behind her is fluttering in the soft breeze. Purchased in 1916.

45 HENRI DE TOULOUSE-LAUTREC
(b. 1864, Albi–d. 1901, Malromé):
Ces Dames! 1894
Pastel crayon on cardboard, 60.3 × 80.5 cm
The full title of the picture is *These Ladies in the Dining Room,* and it portrays Lautrec's favourite models, the inmates of a "distinguished" brothel. With a clever trick of composition, the subjects are reflected in a mirror in the background. The characters are the same as those in the painting *In the Salon* in the Albi Museum (painted in 1895). Purchased in 1913.

46 VINCENT VAN GOGH
(b. 1853, Groot Zundert–d. 1890, Auvers-sur-Oise):
Provençal Haystack. 1888
India ink and pen, 24.1 × 31.9 cm
A similar drawing was once in Henri Matisse's possession. The composition is nearly identical with a painting of the same subject in the Kröller-Müller Collection. From the Majovszky collection.

47 OSKAR KOKOSCHKA
(b. 1886, Pöchlarn–d. 1981, Villeneuve):
Veronica. 1911
Oil on canvas, 119 × 80 cm
One of the main works of the painter's early period. Kokoschka converts the biblical subject into an imaginative vision; the profound psychological observations and expressiveness are typical of his style. The recognitions of modern psychology and the traditional requisites of the subject are combined into an entirely new, complex pictorial fabric. Purchased in 1964.

48 MARC CHAGALL (b. 1889, Vitebsk–):
Blue Village. 1968
Gouache, 57.6 × 67 cm
Although the painter has been living in France for several decades, his compositions still reflect his childhood experiences, his anguish and vividly whirling dreams—the figures of bearded, caftaned Jews straying forlornly among the wooden houses of the Russian provincial town, and the donkeys and mules in fantastic colours, endowed with virtually human qualities, all enveloped in the pale light of a visionary moon. Purchased in 1972.

49 PABLO PICASSO
(b. 1881, Malaga–d. 1973, Mougins):
Mother and Child. *c.* 1905
India ink and water-colour, 35.3 × 25.3 cm
A pencil sketch for the delicate water colour is in the Fogg Art Museum at Harvard University. A present from Ferenc Hatvany, in 1918.

Hungarian National Gallery

The Hungarian National Gallery collects and preserves works related to Hungary, ranging from Romanesque stone carvings to present-day objects of genre which are increasingly difficult to categorize.

After an early history of some 150 years, the Gallery was founded in 1957, as an organic link in the history of Hungarian museums and art collections.

In 1808, when the National Assembly (Parliament) passed a Bill on the foundation of the country's first museum, Count Ferenc Széchényi had already offered his collection of books, coins and heraldic devices to the nation. When the National Museum was opened in 1847, its collection already included the first Hungarian works of art: István Ferenczy's *Shepherdess* and a portrait of Ferenc Kölcsey, which were the presents from the Palatine Archduke Joseph, one of the most ardent supporters of the cause of Hungarian museums.

In 1836 the state purchased the Jankovich collection, some of whose pieces formed the basis of the collection of old Hungarian masters. There emerged a nation-wide movement urging the establishment of the museum, and the collection of objects of art in general, and several members of the bourgeoisie and the aristocracy made donations and presents to further this goal. The first objects were entered in a joint inventory with the contents of the Department of Antiquities, but by the mid-nineteenth century the considerable growth of indigenous material called for the separation of the Gallery within the National Museum, and by 1851, the setting up of an individual National Gallery.

The National Gallery was the predecessor of the Hungarian National Gallery. Among the intellectual and material driving forces involved in the work of collection were the Pest Art Society, founded in 1840, and the Gallery Society, set up in 1845; in 1861 the two bodies were united to form the National Association of Fine Arts.

By the second half of the nineteenth century, the initial unmethodical manner of acquisition, relying mainly on donations, was replaced by systematic collection. The Gallery tried to acquire major works by notable masters, and upon the suggestion of Ágoston Kubinyi, the second director of the National Museum, information about Hungarian artists were also collected. Plans and rules were worked out for a deliberate enlargement of the collections, with an eye on artistic and cultural history considerations.

That concept is borne out by the first bulletins of the National Gallery, which bear authentic witness to the conditions that prevailed on 21 January 1863. Bulletin No. 1 lists the "portraits worthy of being entered in the inventory". They include János Donát's portraits of Ferenc Kölcsey and Benedek Virág, Miklós Barabás's portraits of Béni Egressy and Ferenc Liszt, and Alajos Györgyi Giergl's portrait of Ferenc Erkel.

Bulletin No. 2 lists oil paintings of various subjects considered "of lasting value". The list gives the names of the donors and the exact dates of acquisition. These details also indicate the eagerness and social activity which helped to search for and acquire the very best pieces of Hungarian painting. These canvases still form the basis of the nineteenth-century exhibition in the Hungarian National Gallery.

Sándor Wagner's picture, *Titus Dugovics,* was a present from a ladies' association in 1861;

Miklós Barabás's *A Wandering Rumanian Family* was presented by the Hungarian Civic Guard of Pest, while Bálint Kiss's *The Farewell of János Jablonczai Pethes* came to the Museum in 1848 as a present from the landowner Zsigmond Kovács. Viktor Madarász's *The Bewailing of László Hunyadi*, Károly Markó's *Ideal Landscape* and Mór Than's *The Arrest of Nyári and Pekry* were purchased by the Gallery Society and presented to the Museum.

Bulletin No. 3. contains pictures "to be discarded". They include Károly Kisfaludy's *Night Storm.*

Bulletin No. 4 lists "unarranged" and "anonymous" pictures.

The first pieces in the collection of sculptures included István Ferenczy's legacy, presented to the Museum by Mrs András Jánosdeák, and Miklós Izsó's legacy, which the Museum purchased from his studio.

Miklós Izsó's sculpture, *The Grieving Shepherd,* came to the collection as the donation of an industrialist in 1864. The Markó pictures were acquired on several occasions. The first, *The Treasures of the Holy Past,* was part of the Pyrker collection. Later Ágoston Kubinyi canvassed for subscriptions to a fund, out of which five Markó pictures were purchased, and finally eight more canvases were bought from the painter's residual estate, the money for which was again collected by subscription.

The incorporation of the truly outstanding aristocratic and church collections did not add greatly to the quality of Hungarian works.

Along with the Jankovich and the Pyrker collections, the largest expansion came from the purchase of the Esterházy Gallery. This huge collection is of an encyclopaedic nature, but only included a few works by Hungarian artists, among them Ádám Mányoki's portrait of the Prince of Saxony August II, and a canvas by József Borsos, *Girls after the Ball.*

The 1848 government confiscated the treasures in the residence of the chairman of the Buda treasury, including 76 oils, but these enriched the collection of the General Gallery.

By the end of the last century, Hungarian art was gaining increasing recognition. The rapid growth in the number of objects and the continuous flow of presents led to a situation where the National Museum could no longer provide adequate room for a well-arranged display of the material, and not even for its storage. It is true that in 1871 the National Gallery was set up in the Academy of Sciences, but it could house little more than the works of art from the Esterházy Gallery. The two institutions also exchanged some of their objects, with pictures by Hungarian painters and more recent paintings taken to the National Museum in exchange for works by old foreign masters to be displayed in the Academy.

By the last years of the nineteenth century, there was a definite demand for a separate, new museum to house the collection of fine arts, so that the National Museum should only display, together with its other material, a Gallery of Historical Portraits.

The Millenary Act at long last brought the Museum of Fine Arts into being. By 1892, four years before the ruling, the "register books were closed" in the National Museum, and according to their figures the Pyrker Gallery included 192 objects, the General Gallery 355 and the Hungarian Gallery 555 registered pieces.

In 1896, the year of the millenary celebrations, an Art Council was formed, which, together with the Purchasing Committee that was set up somewhat later, had the task of buying objects for the new museum then under construction. It was during that preparatory period that Master M.S.'s *Visitation* was acquired by the museum, and so were Pál Szinyei Merse's *Picnic in May,* the Gothic High Altar from Kisszeben (now Sabinov, Czechoslovakia), as well as some pictures by Jakab Bogdány, which were presented to the museum by Marcell Nemes. In 1900, the material was enriched by 11 Munkácsy pictures.

The Museum of Fine Arts was opened in 1906. The backbone of its collection came from the National Gallery and the National Museum, and it was later enlarged with presents from private collectors such as the Majovszky and the Pálffy collections.

A further enrichment of the Museum's objects both in number, spirit and novel character, came with the purchases by the Directorate during the 1919 Hungarian Soviet Republic. Two female nudes by József Nemes Lampérth formed part of the new acquisitions.

In the first half of the present century the Museum of Fine Arts went through its most brilliant period under the directorship of Elek Petrovics. The twenty years of his activity became closely connected with the history of the museum and of Hungarian fine arts. Petrovics had a well-considered policy of collection, he inspired donors and ensured a proper status for objects that up till the time had been despised or neglected. Instead of occasional purchases, he laid the foundations for a systematic, scholarly collection. The salvaging of diptychs and triptychs and Baroque sculptures, which had been formerly considered valueless, also dates from those years.

Petrovics attempted to complete the nineteenth-century material by purchasing pictures by Bertalan Székely, László Paál and Mihály Munkácsy, and he also promoted the art of the *fin de siècle*. He purchased major works by Pál Szinyei Merse, József Rippl-Rónai and Károly Ferenczy to enable a monographic presentation of their art.

He mounted annual exhibitions to display the latest acquisitions, and the scholarly processing of the collections also gained impetus during his directorship.

The years after the Second World War again favoured the further enlargement of the existing collections. Objects treated as deposits, which later were unclaimed, became the Museum's property, and the treasures of war victims and people who left the country also came into state ownership. Some major private collections, for example the Wolfner and the Fettich collections, were also added to the Museum's material after the country's liberation. Despite the huge exhibition space offered by the imposing dimensions of the Museum of Fine Arts, the valuable art works of foreign masters and the plaster casts in the ground-floor hall left no proper room for the Hungarian works, and it was impossible within the frames of periodic or temporary exhibitions to gauge the development and values of Hungarian art and to present the works for scholarly analysis in a chronological order, or at least to classify them according to varoius schools. Elek Petrovics was the first to look for some solution when he organized a permanent display of twentieth-century works in the old Art Gallery, but even that did not solve the presentation of the full range of Hungarian painting. That led to a state of affairs in which the establishment of a new museum became a pressing necessity.

The decision to found the Hungarian National Gallery was reached in 1953. As a first step towards that goal, the Budapest City Art Gallery had been merged with the Museum of Fine Arts, so as to have the collections of the two museums as the basis for the very first independent gallery of Hungarian works.

The Budapest City Art Gallery was founded in 1933 to display the material the capital city had collected from the 1880s onwards. The initial aim was to support young artists; later on, to collect works related to Budapest, and finally a special committee was set up to purchase pictures from exhibitions, more and more disregarding thematic restrictions.

The capital assumed the role of a patron, the pictures purchased were mainly put up in office rooms, and in 1924, in honour of the 50th anniversary of the unification of Pest and Buda, they were displayed at a large exhibition. Some of the paintings did not come up to the standards required of a museum exhibit, but the majority formed later worthy additions to the material of the Museum of Fine Arts. The more so, as before the war, the two museums agreed to divide the field of collection between themselves. The Budapest City Art Gallery was functioning as an independent institution for two decades, during which time it acquired some real masterpieces, such as the *Portrait of Mme Bittó* and *Pigeon-Post* by Miklós Barabás, *The Letter* by József Borsos, *Dalmatian Seashore* by Tivadar Csontváry Kosztka, *Isola Bella* by József Egry and *The Rákóczi March* by Simon Hollósy. The material also included works by Mányoki and Bogdány, and among its more recent acquisitions were the finest works by Derkovits, Dési Huber and Róbert Berény. After the Second World War, the Budapest City Art Gallery was the first institution in Budapest to mount an exhibition in the Károlyi mansion.

The four years that followed the merger of the Budapest City Art Gallery and the Museum of Fine Arts were spent with the restoration and preparation of the collections, until finally on 5 October 1957, the Hungarian National Gallery was opened in the building of the former Royal Supreme Court, rebuilt to house the museum. During the first year 6,000 paintings, 2,100 sculptures and 3,100 coins were handed over from the Museum of Fine Arts, with the collection of graphic works following the next year.

The first exhibition in the Gallery was intended to represent the history of Hungarian painting rather than individual works. A floor each was taken up by exhibitions of nineteenth and twentieth-century painting. The sculptures were placed in the entrance hall and along the corridors. The works of old Hungarian masters remained in the Museum of Fine Arts, most of them in the store rooms, waiting for a permanent exhibition.

The rooms on the ground floor of the former Supreme Court housed temporary exhibitions every two to three months.

The enlargement of the stock of objects has been determined by the practice introduced after the country's liberation in 1945. Purchases from the Gallery's own financial resources were supplemented with purchases by the Ministry of Culture and the Art Fund, and with the long-standing tradition of donations.

The New Hungarian Picture Gallery was enriched in the first year of its existence by some major works by Derkovits (*The Enforcement Order, Boilersmith, Concert*). Albert Tikos's picture, *Before Bathing*, and a picture by Elek Szamossy, the one-time master of Munkácsy, were acquired at an auction. The years 1959 and 1960 brought one of the most successful periods in the history of collecting at the Gallery. Entries in the inventory included a *Self-portrait* by Munkácsy, Viktor Madarász's *Dobozi*, László Paál's *Sheep-pens*, Adolf Fényes's *Small Town Street*, Károly Ferenczy's *October* and his *Archers*, and Károly Kernstok's *Riders on the Shore*, and the pictures were put on display immediately. The Department of Sculpture had been enriched, among other pieces, with a bronze copy of János Pásztor's *Rákóczi*, Alajos Stróbl's *Martinovics* bust and Miklós Borsos's portrait of Lőrinc Szabó, while new acquisitions of the Department of Drawings and Prints included Mihály Zichy's *Scottish Hunters* and Jenő Barcsay's series, *Man and Drapery*.

Gyula Benczúr's *Reading Woman* has been recovered from Munich, Munkácsy's *The Condemned Cell* from Paris, his *Colpach School* from Yugoslavia, and his sketch-books from Hanover, Zichy's *Faust* illustrations from Rome, and his drawing, *Jewish Martyrs*, from Moscow. The 117 drawings by Lajos Tihanyi have been a present from Brassai, the famous photographer and art dealer in Paris.

In 1961 the Gallery purchased the residual estate of Imre Ámos. The legacies of Bertalan Pór, János Vaszary, Ernő Schubert and Noémi Ferenczy also brought major enlargements, mainly for the Department of Drawings and Prints.

In 1959, two years after the opening of the Hungarian National Gallery, a government decree allocated the final place for the Gallery in the former Royal Palace in Buda.

The planning of the post-war reconstruction of the palace began in 1960–61, taking into account the requirements for the museum. Royal residences had been put to similar use in a number of European capitals: the Louvre in Paris, the Hermitage in Leningrad, the Vienna Hofburg and the Escorial in Madrid now all house works of art. The large rooms, halls and wide corridors are particularly suitable for housing museums and representative exhibitions. The Royal Palace in Buda has three museums within its walls, each with ample space for exhibition and storage. The Hungarian National Gallery was given the three central buildings in the wing facing the Danube. Some fifteen years passed from the time of the first designs until in 1974–75 the museum could occupy its final place. Today the country's national art has found its final home on three floors and several corridors of the former Royal Palace.

The diptychs and triptychs are displayed in the former throne-room, and the medieval panels and sculptures in the Gothic halls on the ground floor. The first floor houses the Baroque exhibition, leading without any break to nineteenth-century painting. The large-size historical paintings from the last century can be seen in the ballroom, with pictures by Mihály Munkácsy and László Paál preserved in air-conditioned glass cases. The second and third floors are devoted to twentieth-century painting, beginning with works of the Nagybánya School, through to present-day works. Also on the third floor is an exhibition room for temporary displays of works of graphic art and a "studio" reserved for living artists, which presents various creative processes and some of the most recent works.

The statues are traditionally set up in the larger open spaces and the corridors, with some of them organically incorporated within the theme of the exhibition of paintings. Opposite the main entrance on the ground floor there is a room for temporary exhibitions, retrospective shows, jubilee displays, exchange exhibitions from abroad and comprehensive presentations of various schools or periods. Every second week there are concerts in the cupola hall and the Baroque exhibition halls, and visitors can avail themselves of expert guides. Film shows and lectures serve to promulgate the museum's material, and the artistic relics of several centuries are attended to, processed and treated in publications by art historians and restorers.

This move into the former home of kings has in all probability brought the 150-year-long tribulations of the largest Hungarian public collection to a final conclusion.

Together with its departments of paintings, sculptures and graphic works, the Hungarian National Gallery also plays a significant role in Hungary's cultural life with the presentation and scholarly processing of certain works. In common with other museums in the country, the Gallery plays a growing role in public education as well, organizing concerts, literary evenings, guided tours and various programmes for students. The library stocks a comprehensive bibliography covering the fields of the Gallery's collections.

Zsuzsa Turcsány

DESCRIPTION
OF ILLUSTRATIONS

50 (a) Statue of St Dorothy from Barka. 1410–20
Lime, with traces of paint, 169.5 cm
The statue is the most telling proof of the place occupied by the sculpture of Northern Hungary in fifteenth-century Europe. Together with the statue of St Catherine, it formed part of the altar-piece of the church of Barka (now Bôrka, Czechoslovakia). Even in its present state, with the crown missing and the fragmentary basket, it projects devout beauty and the exceptional talent of its master. The shaping represents the "Soft Style" in the series of "Beautiful Madonnas". The drapery of her dress, the posture of the figure, her high brow and the etherealized expression on her face do not have a counterpart anywhere in Europe—it is undoubtedly the work of a Hungarian sculptor. It came to the Museum of Fine Arts from József Pécsi's collection in 1947.

(b) UPPER HUNGARIAN SCULPTOR:
King Saint Stephen. *c.* 1500–1510
Limewood; height: 114 cm
The figure presumably comes from Mateóc in the Szepesség (Zips) region (now Matejovce, Czechoslovakia), as does the figure of King Saint Ladislas. The majestic figure, carved realistically, is surrounded by High Gothic decorative forms. The statue was transferred to the Museum of Fine Arts from the Hungarian National Museum, between 1936 and 1939.

51 MASTER M.S.:
The Visitation. 1506
Tempera on wood (lime), 140 × 94.5 cm
The painter is only known by his initials, which feature, together with the date 1506, on the picture *Resurrection*, one of six related panels. Four of them *(Resurrection, The Mount of Olives, Christ Carrying the Cross* and *Calvary)* are in the Christian

Museum at Esztergom, while *The Nativity* is preserved in the church of Hontszentantal (now Antol, Czechoslovakia). The six panels once formed the High Altar of Selmecbánya (now Banská Štiavnica, Czechoslovakia), three niche statues of which are still to be found there. *The Visitation,* the visit of Mary to Elisabeth, is the most beatiful piece of the series. The two graceful, delicately fragile Gothic figures are veiled in devout solemnity, with the poetic landscape and the flowers in the foreground as their loveliest ornament, in an encounter with the poetry of motherhood, Gothic mysticism and the landscape. It was acquired during the preparatory period for the Museum of Fine Arts.

52 Madonna with Rose from Kassa.
c. 1500
Tempera on wood (pine) and decorated gold plates, 51 × 41 cm; with frame: 71 × 60.5 cm
By the fifteenth century Kassa (now Košice, Czechoslovakia) became the centre of artistic activity in Northern Hungary. The monumental construction work of the cathedral enabled, and indeed called for, an increase in the number of painter's workshops and these constructing altars. Although by the 1500s, Madonnas all over Europe were already closer to earthly existence, the Kassa Madonna had preserved an aura of hermetic closedness, which only allows mortals to approach her with a mystical worship. In all probability it was the work of a well-versed painter of traditional icons, who endowed his Madonna with the majesty and invulnerability of icons.

53. JAKAB BOGDÁNY
(b. *c.* 1660, Eperjes [now Prešov, Czechoslovakia]–d. 1724, London):
Flower Piece. 1690s
Oil on canvas, 62 × 49 cm
A painter of still-lifes of flowers and pictures of animals, Bogdány was of Hungarian extraction, who later settled in Britain. His patrons included Queen Mary II of England and William III, who commissioned a picture for his castle in the Netherlands. The flowers are painted with minute care, and the atmosphere of the

Netherlands in his flower pieces shows the influence of his studies in Amsterdam. In England his style became further polished according to the taste of the day, and he was said to paint "tittivated fruits". Taken over from the Museum of Fine Arts.

54 ÁDÁM MÁNYOKI
(b. 1673, Szokolya–d. 1757, Dresden):
Self-portrait. 1700–02
Oil on canvas, 87 × 61.5 cm
Ádám Mányoki is best known as the court painter to Prince Ferenc Rákóczi. His Rákóczi portrait is one of the most valuable relics of Hungarian history and art history, but some of his other masterpieces, including his *Self-portrait,* are also worthy of attention. Besides the brocades and jewels painted with Baroque splendour, the most remarkable feature of this painting is its simplicity. It depicts a self-respecting craftsman with his tools, which happen to be the brush and the palette. His jaunty hat, open collar and cheerful expression show an artlessness unusual for the time. Mányoki became later the court painter to the Elector of Saxony. Taken over from the Museum of Fine Arts.

55 KÁROLY MARKÓ THE ELDER
(b. 1791, Lőcse [now Levoča, Czechoslovakia]–d. 1860, Villa Appeggi, Italy):
Visegrád. 1826–30
Oil on canvas, 58.5 × 83 cm
Károly Markó was the first great master of Hungarian landscape painting, whose trend created a school. *Visegrád* is a determinative work from his youth. The landscape is depicted with a remarkable fidelity to detail, and is a fine example of the beginning of "portrait-like landscape painting" in Hungary. Markó later abandoned this trend, and after having settled in Italy, painted academic, idealized landscapes. The Hungarian state did much to regain his pictures. *Visegrád* was purchased by the National Gallery in 1890.

56 MIKLÓS BARABÁS
(b. 1810, Márkusfalva [now Markušovce, Czechoslovakia]–d. 1898, Budapest):
Portrait of Mme Bittó. 1874
Oil on canvas, 84 × 66 cm

Barabás was the father figure of the rising generation of the Reform Age, and for decades he was surrounded with respect and esteem. He painted portraits throughout his career, and the features of many great figures in Hungarian public life and literature have only survived through his brush. The *Portrait of Mme Bittó* originates from his old age, but shows no sign of slackening in his creative ability and expressive force. Mme Bittó is among the finest female portraits. The picture is dominated by the fine, transparent fabric of the dress in the style of the time, which also underlines the hands resting in her lap. The face is softened by the noble arch of the nose and the brows. The high forehead is accentuated by her coiffure to which the painter devoted special care. Purchased by the Budapest City Art Gallery from Baroness Erzsébet Radosevics.

57 BERTALAN SZÉKELY (b. 1835, Kolozsvár [now Cluj-Napoca, Rumania]–d. 1910, Mátyásföld):
Red-haired Girl. 1870s
Oil on canvas, 56.5 × 46.5 cm
A notable, mature and fine piece of Hungarian portraiture. In the full possession of his artistic skill and with his great historical canvases behind him, Székely's attention turned more carefully to subjects of bourgeois life. His sensitive brushwork reproduces faithfully the tender, pale, gloomy face of the little red-haired girl. Beyond the charming pictorial spectacle, the wavy red hair, the wan, freckled skin and the pale eyelashes also present an evocative portrayal of character. The picture was acquired by the Museum of Fine Arts as part of the Wolfner collection.

58 ISTVÁN FERENCZY (b. 1792, Rimaszombat [now Rimavská Sobota, Czechoslovakia]–d. 1856, Rimaszombat):
Shepherdess. 1822
Marble, 94 cm
Also known as "The Beginning of Fine Arts", this work is one of the first major efforts in Hungarian sculpture. The young girl incises the silhouette of her departing sweetheart into the dust, and by so doing, gives birth to the demand for artistic re-

production. Ferenczy modelled the statue during his years of study in Rome, closely adhering to Canova's instructions.

The disciplined, delicately poetic statue, composed for one view, embodies the ideals of Classicism. The sculptor himself presented the work to the Hungarian nation. For some time it stood in the ground-floor hall of the Royal Palace, and the Palatine Archduke Joseph presented it to the National Museum. In 1870, it was taken from the Department of Antiquities to the Gallery, and from there it went to the Museum of Fine Arts in 1907.

59 MIKLÓS IZSÓ
(b. 1831, Disznóshorváti–d. 1875, Budapest):
Dancing Peasant. 1870–71
Terracotta, 20.2 cm
Miklós Izsó's 15 statuettes of dancing peasants in terracotta are displayed in a glass-case in the exhibition of nineteenth-century objects. The are sketches, and perhaps precisely because of that they have a typical freshness and sweep. They are figures formed with an easy hand, like the ancient Tanagra figurines and yet they are typical products of nineteenth-century national folk romanticism, as borne out by the dance motif in this piece, and the characteristic peasant faces. The National Museum acquired the statuette in 1876.

60 LÁSZLÓ MEDNYÁNSZKY
(b. 1862, Beczkó [now Beckov, Czechoslovakia]–d. 1919, Vienna):
Head of a Tramp. 1897
Oil on canvas, 45 × 34.5 cm
A typical subject for Mednyánszky, the somewhat eccentric painter, a born wanderer, who spent his nights at refuges. But its atmospheric charge and grotesque expressiveness raise this picture above his other portrayals of tramps. The face reflects the despair of the outcasts of society, staring with an empty look, mad with hunger or perhaps with a craving for alcohol. The mouth opening as if to cry intensifies the drama of the painting to the utmost. The Museum of Fine Arts acquired it from the estate of Biró Beczkói.

61 MIHÁLY MUNKÁCSY
(b. 1844, Munkács [now Mukachevo, Soviet Union]–d. 1900, Endenich, Germany, [now West Germany]:
Dusty Road. 1874
Oil on wood, 96 × 129.7 cm
A cart is coming along the road lined with dusty trees to the right. The landscape is dominated by the infinite, lowering sky of the Great Hungarian Plain. It seems amazingly new among Munkácsy's landscapes. The opalescent atmosphere recalls the Impressionists, yet the mood and resolved atmosphere do not spring from the new French outlook, but from Munkácsy's realistic pictorial view, the reality of the dust whirling on the road. Munkácsy painted the picture during a visit to Hungary, and the Museum of Fine Arts purchased it from his widow in 1904.

62 PÁL SZINYEI MERSE (b. 1845, Szinye-Újfalu [now Chminianska Nová Ves, Czechoslovakia]–d. 1920, Jernye [now Jarovnice, Czechoslovakia]):
Picnic in May. 1873
Oil on canvas, 127 × 163.5 cm
Szinyei was 27 years old when he painted his masterpiece, *Picnic in May*. The message of the picture is unclouded existence itself in its utter simplicity, devoid of any mystery. Even though the glowing colours radiate the love of nature, Szinyei is still not an Impressionist painter of spectacle, dissolving form. His figures move on the ground of reality and are surrounded by nature's intensified splendour. On a European scale too the picture is among the first gems of plein-air painting. After some twenty years of neglect, the canvas came to the Museum of Fine Arts from the Millenary Exhibition in 1896.

63 KÁROLY FERENCZY
(b. 1862, Vienna–d. 1917, Budapest):
October. 1903
Oil on canvas, 125 × 107 cm
One of the most mature pieces in Hungarian plein-air painting. It encompasses all the achievements of the Nagybánya School, including what is incorporated from Impressionist endeavours. All the components in the composition are grouped around the sunshade which casts a shadow, even on the figure of the man standing with his back to the spectator. The Nagybánya interpretation of nature is expressed here in its purest form. The gorgeous harmony of the changing seasons from summer into autumn is rendered with the proportions of colour range.

Károly Ferenczy was a founder of the Nagybánya artists' colony, being one of its teachers and leading figures, and this most monumental trend in Hungarian painting of the end of the nineteenth century became linked with his name. The Gallery acquired the canvas in 1959 from the Chorin deposit.

64 ALADÁR KÖRÖSFŐI-KRIESCH
(b. 1863, Buda–d. 1920, Budapest):
Study for Klára Zách. 1912
Pastel on paper, 50.2 × 34.6 cm
The delicate pastel figure of a woman is one of a few preparatory studies for the two large-size oils entitled *Klára Zách*. The story of Klára Zách is one of the most blood-stained dramas of the Hungarian Middle Ages, which inspired several noted painters in the nineteenth century as well (Soma Orlai Petrich, Viktor Madarász, Pál Vágó). Körösfői treats the subject in the style of Art Nouveau, bringing the external marks of the plot to the fore. The magic of the exquisite garments, elegant, dignified gestures and the captivating mood make the historical fact of the brutal murder even more appalling. The drawing was purchased by the Museum of Fine Arts.

65 LAJOS GULÁCSY
(b. 1882, Budapest–d. 1932, Budapest):
Paolo and Francesca. 1903
Pencil and water-colour on paper, 33.1 × 25.2 cm
A rare piece of clear lines and fully drawn work even in Gulácsy's life work. His attraction to Italian Renaissance is apparent both in the manner of drawing and the choice of subject. Dante's two lovers doomed to the Inferno are portrayed with a compassionate, sweet lyricism. The background of a typically Italian landscape expresses the mood of the imaginary period, and the relationship between Paolo and

Francesca suggests the eternal rapture of love. The sheet was purchased by the Museum of Fine Arts in 1907.

66 JÓZSEF RIPPL-RÓNAI
(b. 1861, Kaposvár–d. 1927, Kaposvár):
Father and Uncle Piacsek Drinking Red Wine. 1907
Oil and crayon on cardboard, 69 × 100 cm
A typically decorative, stylized, so-called mosaic painting, radiating the warmth of family life and the painter's emotional links with the two men represented. Rippl-Rónai studied in Paris and belonged, also through his friends and links with fellow artists, to the European vanguard of the day; the painting is one of the most mature pieces of his fruitful period in Hungary, which produced many outstanding pieces. Elek Petrovics purchased the picture for the Museum of Fine Arts in 1929.

67 LAJOS TIHANYI
(b. 1885, Budapest–d. 1938, Paris):
Portrait of Lajos Fülep. 1915
Oil on canvas, 77.5 × 95 cm
A self-educated painter of Kassák's circle, Lajos Tihanyi was a founding member of the group known as The Eight. The model of the portrait is the art philosopher and aesthete Lajos Fülep, editor of the periodical *Szellem*, and a university professor after Hungary's liberation in 1945. It is a typical Tihanyi portrait, at the meeting-point of Cubism and Expressionism. The analytical brush dismembers the forms of the body and sets them in motion, but the marks of affection and respect concentrated in the face provide the unity of character. The picture was presented to the Gallery in 1970 by Brassai the photographer.

68 TIVADAR CSONTVÁRY KOSZTKA
(b. 1853, Kisszeben [now Sabinov, Czechoslovakia]–d. 1919, Budapest):
Ruins of the Greek Theatre at Taormina. 1904–05
Oil on canvas, 302 × 570 cm
The passion of this most passionate of painters is only surpassed by his absolute adherence to reality. He paints the columns and gates of the theatre with minute care; the small ships rocking in the bay, the

houses of the bourgeoisie and the infinite horizon with its bold, compelling prisms of colour, all find their place in the canvas, and yet the composition is held together by the cohesive force of Csontváry's burning genius. The "unity of the Greek theatre with nature" has been reestablished in Csontváry's monumental picture. The painting is listed as a deposit in the Hungarian National Gallery.

69 JÓZSEF NEMES LAMPÉRTH (b. 1891, Budapest–d. 1924, Sátoraljaújhely):
Female Nude from the Back. 1916
Oil on canvas, 128 × 77 cm
The body, as built out of geometrical forms with vigorous strokes, has a sculptural effect. The contrast between the accentuated white spots and the deep red of the shadows lends it a dramatic force, creating, together with the statuesque forms, a static character and striking tautness. The painter belonged to the Activists rallying round Kassák's periodical *MA*, and during his sadly short creative period was one of the most remarkable avant-garde painters. The picture, together with its companion piece, also a nude, came to the Museum of Fine Arts as part of the purchases made by the Directorate during the Hungarian Soviet Republic in 1919.

70 JÓZSEF EGRY
(b. 1893, Újlak–d. 1951, Badacsonytomaj):
Badacsony Lights (Golden Gate).
1943–44
Tempera and pastel on paper,
110 × 140 cm
József Egry was a worthy painter of the Hungarian landscape, mainly of the lights of Lake Balaton. The hills and the water only serve as tools to express his immense love for light. His individual form of idiom retained the outlook of Impressionism, but also expressed the drama of inner struggles. Egry spent almost all his life in voluntary exile at Lake Balaton. The picture was presented to the Museum of Fine Arts by the Ministry of Culture in 1947.

71 Gyula Derkovits
(b. 1894, Szombathely–d. 1934, Budapest):
Mother. 1934
Tempera on canvas, 64.5 × 56 cm
The last picture by Derkovits is a synthesis of affection and social message. A necessarily lyrical picture, with a lyrical realm of colour. It fits organically into the painter's life work, virtually crowning its emotional saturation and his temperamental adherence to true values and transforming them into masterpieces. The work-worn hand of the mother embraces the child softly, offering security, her eyes reflect concentrated love. The two overlapping heads prove their affinity more eloquently than words could do. The picture was purchased by the Budapest City Art Gallery in 1952 from Lajos Fruchter.

72 Béla Kondor (b. 1931, Pestszentlő-rinc–d. 1972, Budapest):
The Genius of Mechanical Flight. 1964
Oil on canvas, 230 × 187 cm
Flying for Béla Kondor had a similar meaning to what it meant to the poet Attila József: "If I close my eyes, aeroplanes do crash, even those which get off within me day by day." (Attila József "Keserű" [Bitter, 1925]). The cloud-bodied angel with its meek, lovely face just releases a flying machine, with a steam locomotive of Stephenson's time puffing along on the ground as a counterpoint. A sailing boat is lying on the horizon, and the stoker throws coal on a tiny angel. Can such a fervour for contrivances be believed of Kondor, or does he, here too, poke fun with an affectionate grimace, at conventional human rapture? The Hungarian National Gallery acquired the picture in 1972 as part of the painter's estate.

Museum of Applied Arts

The Budapest Museum of Applied Arts was founded in 1872, as one of the first museums of its kind in Europe, after the comparable institutions in Britain, Austria and Germany. That type of museum did not grow out of aristocratic collections like its fellow institutions, but was created everywhere in response to social demand.

The 1851 World Exhibition in London already demonstrated the backwardness and non-competitiveness of craftsmanship in comparison with the rapid advance of manufacturing industry. A way out of the aesthetic deterioration of articles in daily use seemed to be to combine industry with art, to create an up-to-date, high-standard environment with adequate objects to furnish it. The idea met with a favourable response, as to raise the aesthetic appreciation of everyday objects seemed to be the solution for raising the culture of living standards. The new concept of "applied art" became generally known and by the second half of the nineteenth century, the furthering of applied arts became a new, typical feature of the artistic scene. Museums, schools and societies were founded to preserve the values of handicraft.

The movement started in Britain and soon spread to the Continent. In Hungary the word "applied art" was first put to paper by Lajos Kossuth, a leading politician and statesman, in his report on the Exhibition of Works of Applied Art, in 1842. Arnold Ipolyi, Flóris Rómer and Ferenc Pulszky, in their capacity of museum directors, saw the social significance of the new concept and the possibilities inherent in it, and fought for its popularization. In Flóris Rómer's words, they aimed "with words and deeds" to establish an institution to house applied arts. Their endeavours met with success when the Hungarian National Assembly in 1872 allocated 50,000 forints for the foundation of the institution and for purchases at the Vienna World Exhibition.

From the beginning of its existence, the new museum attracted attention with a number of new features; it established Hungarian and international relations, and showed keen interest in contemporary applied arts. The basic idea behind its activity was that the life of modern man calls for a modern environment as one of its prerequisites, and applied art and its museum have a decisive role in its development.

The committee sent to the Vienna World Exhibition in 1873 purchased modern objects of applied arts; it also acquired Prince Wittgenstein's collection of antique vessels and the Fischbach collection of textiles. The material collected by János Xántus during his expedition to Eastern Asia in 1869–70 also came to the Museum. Later Hungarian objects of applied art and folk art were also acquired. The stocks were further enlarged with private donations, and the Museum soon outgrew its transitional homes. (First it was housed in the National Museum, and later in the old Art Gallery.)

The first successes came under the directorships of Károly Pulszky and György Ráth. Under Ráth the Museum's statutes and inventories were drawn up, and the first trade exhibition mounted. Since 1878 the Museum has featured in the state budget.

In 1887 Jenő Radisics became the director, and his management opened a flourishing chapter in the Museum's history. He set up methodical arrangements within the Museum and promoted foreign relations. Even before him, the Museum took part at the exhibition of the Vienna Museum of Applied Arts in 1883 and at the exhibitions of the Union Centrale des Arts Decoratifs in Paris in 1882 and 1884, but Radisics further intensified international contacts. The Museum enriched its material with purchases at the Paris World Exhibition in 1900 and at several auctions abroad. Of the purchases and valuable presents originating in Hungary, mention should be made of Imre Szalay's collection, the large collection of Hungarian glazed earthenware of Bishop Zsigmond Bubits and Mrs György Ráth's benefaction.

To complement Jenő Radisics's many innovations, his greatest achievement was the establishment of the final building for the Museum and School of Applied Arts, an object for which he fought passionately. The state purchased the necessary ground in 1890, and invited tenders for the designs of the building. The competition was won by the plans of Ödön Lechner and Gyula Pártos.

During the construction work, Radisics visited several large museums of fine arts in Europe, studying their equipment, arrangements and working methods. He was mostly impressed by the organizational work and equipment of the South Kensington Museum in London (today Victoria and Albert Museum), and he applied the lessons he drew there to several features of the Budapest museum. Several details of the building and its equipment still show the influence of the London museum. The Museum was opened during the millenary celebrations, on 25 October 1896, by King and Emperor Francis Joseph I.

The same building houses the Museum of Applied Arts and part of the College of Applied Arts today.

The new museum soon became popular in Hungary and gained recognition abroad. The building itself has given rise to a mixture of recognition and criticism. Criticism was levelled on the overall effect of the building designed to meet Art Nouveau tastes, amalgamating many different influences, including Hungarian trends; but even the critics acknowledged the monumental architectural solutions of some of its details.

Up till the First World War, the contents of the Museum were enlarged with several purchases, bequests and donations, as for example Zsigmond Bubits's bequest, presents from Imre Szalay, Frigyes Glück, Marcell Nemes, Mrs György Ráth and Baroness Lipthay, and the Delhaes bequest. Besides exhibitions of the various collections of the Museum, several memorable foreign displays were also held, for example the Walter Crane Exhibition in 1900, the International Ex Libris Exhibition in 1903 and the successful exhibitions of Swedish and Japanese applied arts. The Museum also made purchases at auctions abroad, such as the 1884 Gedon auction in Munich and the 1893 Spitzer auction in Paris.

The educational lectures at the Museum drew large audiences. But the First World War checked this development, and the post-war years brought a slackening in further acquisitions. The period is also marked by valuable exhibitions and publications, but shrinking subsidies, the deterioration of the building and other deficiencies increasingly made themselves felt. In 1922, the Museum became part of the National Hungarian Universal Collections, which included several museums, and in 1934 was reorganized into the National Museum. Within this framework the Museum of Applied Arts lost its independence, and the regrouping of the objects also meant losses in its collections.

Major exhibitions were still held in that period too: Art Treasures of Transylvania (1923), Oriental Rugs (1924), Church Art, and displays of watches and tapestry (1926), silverware (1927) and laces (1933), all with illustrated catalogues. The valuable bequests and presents included those from Mrs Procopius (1927), Mrs Perlep (1927) and the wife of Baron József Hatvany (1928).

During the Second World War the museum building suffered grave damage, and by the time of the country's liberation in 1945, both the building and the collections were in a poor state.

The first post-war years were devoted to the tremendous task of the country's reconstruction. In a few years' time the Museum was also renovated, and it embarked on a new path of development, based on its organizational independence, expanding staff and new financial provisions.

In 1947, the Museum was expanded by a co-institution, the Ferenc Hopp Museum of Eastern Asiatic Art, part of whose material was exhibited as the Chinese Museum in the former villa of György Ráth, which his widow presented to the Museum of Applied Arts in 1905. In 1948, Géza Dáni offered the Baroque mansion at Nagytétény with its beautiful frescoes to the Museum. After proper renovations the mansion has housed various exhibitions, such as the one on the history of furniture. The Museum's collection of stoves and tiles is also exhibited there (today: Nagytétény Castle Museum, Budapest, 22nd District).

Even under the difficult conditions after the Second World War, the Museum tried to perform its assignments. In 1946, to mark the 50th anniversary of its existence, the exhibition "Masterworks of the Museum of Applied Arts" was opened and a guide published. That was followed by a number of displays. Growing state support allowed for a marked enlargement of the collections, while the larger number of staff members led to growing scholarly and cultural achievements. The most important of the many bequests and donations include the collection of ceramics of Professor Vince Wartha, the international collection of ceramics of more recent times of Professor Ottó Fettick, the collection of ex-libris and small-scale graphic works of Academician Rezső Soó, and the valuable private collection of Ferenc Papolczy and his wife.

The Museum continues to extend its sphere of interests to many new fields. Improving conditions allow for improving work. The collections have been arranged into groups, and the material is stored in adequate repositories. The objects are preserved in the departments of the Museum in groupings according to their material. Every department has its own conservation workshop, with qualified restorers looking after the material. The collections consist of Hungarian and foreign works of applied art, mainly from the sixteenth century to the present day.

In 1972 the Museum marked the 100th anniversary of its foundation with an exhibition, issuing a richly illustrated catalogue and organizing festive programmes. By that time the number of its objects exceeded 60,000. The various departments are as follows:

FURNITURE DEPARTMENT. Recent years brought a considerable extension of the material. It preserves valuable Gothic, Italian Renaissance as well as French and Central European Baroque pieces. Outstanding in the material are the systematically collected French Baroque, Rococo and Neo-Classical signed pieces of furniture, many by noted cabinet-makers, which were displayed in exhibitions. Together with the large number of Italian, German and Austrian specimens, English furniture is represented by a small but select collection. There is a very rich collection of Hungarian furniture from the seventeenth century onwards. Several suites were set up in the Museum, as for example an eighteenth-century Jesuit pharmacy from Kőszeg (today in the Kőszeg Pharmacy Museum), and the furnishings of the episcopal library of Sümeg. The painted, coffered church ceilings are fine examples of old Hungarian ornamentation, and the valuable old church stalls exemplify furniture-making. A beautiful, varied collection presents empire and Biedermeier style furniture. The Museum also collects more recent and modern material, objects in the style of Historism, from the end of the nineteenth century, and Art Nouveau, early twentieth-century and present-day pieces. Among the valuable pieces which by now count as rarities, are some typical, signed specimens of the early English Art Nouveau, the by now classical relics of French Art Nouveau and early Hungarian pieces from the same period.

In accordance with conservation considerations, objects carved of various woods, including statuettes, are also preserved in the Furniture Department. The material is complemented with a collection of musical instruments, including some signed French harps. Moulds of artistic value also form part of the Department: blue-dyeing patterns and carved honeycake moulds. The latter include many dated pieces from the seventeenth century, with multi-figured compositions. The number of items in the Department is 4,000.

DEPARTMENT OF GOLDSMITH'S AND METAL WORKS. This embraces all types of objects made of precious and base metals. Most valuable are the Hungarian and German (mainly Augsburg and Nuremberg) silver and silver-gilt works from the sixteenth and seventeenth centuries, Renaissance and Baroque dishes, cutlery and centre-pieces, including objects of ivory set in precious metal, of semi-precious stones, shell and coconut. The largest single complex material came from the valuable Esterházy collection. The pieces of applied art from the Esterházy family's treasury came to the Museum after the Second World War: goldsmith's works, jewels, garments, saddles and embroideries. During the Second World War, the collection was in the family's Buda palace and suffered grave damage during the military operations. The pieces are being continuously restored in the Museum.

Nineteenth-century Neo-Classicism is represented by pieces reflecting the tastes of the Hungarian, Austrian, Russian, German and French bourgeoisie. Of special value are the collection of sixteenth to nineteenth-century jewels and gems, the collection of enamels embracing all relevant techniques and the collection of clocks and watches. The latter includes seventeenth-century tower-shaped clocks, travelling clocks and cupboard clocks, and eighteenth-century French, German, Dutch and Flemish gold and enamelled pocket watches.

The bronze collection comprises old Hungarian church equipment, a collection of Italian Renaissance statuettes, and French and Viennese gilded bronze ornamental vessels.

The collection of wrought and cast iron, copper and pewter utensils shows the many-sided development of material culture.

Joined to the Department is a special group of Eastern Slav metal objects, preserving valuable relics of the specific culture of these peoples who settled in Hungary. This culture has produced valuable art objects in this country.

The number of items preserved in the Department amounts to around 10,400.

DEPARTMENT OF CERAMICS AND GLASSWARE. The largest collection of the Museum with about 26,000 pieces. The collection of faience ware boasts seventeenth-century Hungarian Haban pieces and eighteenth-century products of the Holics faience factory, as well as Spanish-Moorish, Italian, German, French and Netherlandish pieces, and objects from the Near East.

Pottery is represented by seventeenth-century German Renaissance jugs, while stone-ware by the Wedgwood Collection and a rich Hungarian and international collection.

The collection of porcelains comprises products of many European manufactures. Its most valuable part is a Viennese collection, of more than 1,000 items, and specimens from Meissen, Nymphenburg, St Petersburg, Sèvres, Herend and Regécz, with early Meissen and early Herend pieces as the *pièces de résistance*.

Mirrors, table sets and a large collection of stoves as well as stove, wall and floor tiles represent early relics of ceramics.

The glass collection contains artistic ancient and medieval glasses (both Oriental and European), blown Venetian, Dutch and old Hungarian glass, as well as carved and ground German, Bohemian, Russian and Hungarian glass. Of outstanding value is the international collection of Art Nouveau glasses.

DEPARTMENT OF TEXTILES. Its collections embrace a wide field both in space and time. The oldest pieces are Coptic textile dress ornaments from the fourth to the seventh centuries. The bulk of the material consists of sixteenth to nineteenth-century Oriental rugs from all the old centres of the craft. From the same centuries there is also a collection of mainly Italian and French damasks, brocades, velvets and fabrics.

Outstanding among the pieces of embroidery is the rich group of old Hungarian and European embroideries. Most widely known are the Italian, Flemish, German and French tapestries. These masterworks, woven according to noble Gothic, Renaissance and Baroque traditions, and some of them linked with historical events, have also attracted attention at exhibitions abroad.

Worthy of attention is a group of Venetian, Brussels and old Hungarian lacework, and the textiles made with different printing techniques, dating from the fifteenth century to the present day, are also of interest.

The valuable collection of costumes and accessories is complete with shoes, hats, gloves, undergarments and bags.

The Department has 26,000 items.

It should be mentioned here, although it holds true of all the departments, that folk variants of the objects are preserved in other museums.

MISCELLANEOUS COLLECTIONS. They embrace collections of varied, valuable articles, such as the collection of ivory (and other bone) carvings, including Romanesque and Gothic pieces, mainly from Italian and French workshops.

The collection of leather tapestries and other old leather work, for example furniture with leather upholstery, are also prized pieces of the Museum, but the most valuable section of the Department is a collection of book bindings or book art, which contains a number of eminent pieces from the fifteenth century to the present day. Many rare types and techniques of the art of book binding can be studied in the collection, and based on the experience gained here, the Museum's restorers have saved many beautiful, irreplaceable codices from destruction in the country.

Of less importance are the collections of fans, étuis, wax pictures and bead-works, yet they have their own place in cultural history. The collections of playing-cards, straw-works, so-called monastic objects, boxes and inner book covers, as well as several other special collections preserving the customs of former times, should also be listed here.

These collections hold 5,100 items.

The work of the departments is assisted by the record office, the library and the documentation section, which are also at the disposal of visitors.

The record office keeps the inventories and the files with the data and photographs of the objects.

The public library is the only place in the country which collects special literature on applied arts. Its stock of 40,000 volumes and periodicals is constantly extended. The library regularly exchanges publications with the major applied arts museums of the world.

The documentation section grew out of the Museum's library, and it also serves as photographic archive. This now separate section collects and preserves much comprehensive material. Its main assignment is to collect and preserve all the documents needed for scholarly research on the history of applied arts. Accordingly, most of the material consists of photographs and negatives, various documents, drawings, designs, manuscripts and posters. The section also stores the Museum's old records, archives, wood-blocks and the like. It also houses a collection of small-scale graphic works and drawings: old greeting cards, postcards, newspaper cuttings, ex-libris, and articles referring to the Museum and its staff members.

New sections called forth by the new tasks are the information section and a section dealing with modern applied arts.

The Museum's activity has been expanded by a number of objectives. In the past attention was mainly focused on handicrafts and the applied arts, but it has been increasingly extended to the present developments in applied arts: the latest achievements in industrial art and design. The progressive trends and methods in the research of the history of applied arts are primarily directed to the processing of the collections. The Museum publishes a periodical under the title *Ars Decorativa*.

The Museum collects and displays at regular exhibitions the latest works of applied artists.

One of the main aims of the Museum is to raise the standard of public education, by lectures, guided tours and concerts in the Museum, and exhibitions in the countryside, and also by establishing relations with factories and schools. The public role of the Museum is enhanced by its regular contacts with church and secular collections and the national supervision of the collections and of research work in applied arts.

The Museum's material features with growing frequency at exhibitions abroad, and the Museum itself also displays the collections of foreign museums.

The Museum keeps pace with international progress in relevant disciplines, something which becomes more and more clearly expressed in its work of research, collection, public education and conservation.

Piroska Weiner

DESCRIPTION OF ILLUSTRATIONS

73 SHAKA NYORAI:
Buddha. "Dry Lacquer" Statue.
8th century A. D.
Height: 44.9 cm
The statue dates fom the Nara period (645–794), the first golden age of Japanese sculpture. Sculpture played a dominant role in art, which at the time meant exclusively religious art. In style it followed the art of the Tang period in China, also taking over technical processes from China. Together with bronze and wood, in the eighth century clay and lacquer appeared for a short time in sculpture. The dry lacquer process reached its artistic perfection in Japan. The essence of the process was to press several layers of bands of linen, saturated with lacquer, into a clay mould. After drying, the more delicate details of the statue's surface were shaped with further layers of lacquer, polished and painted or gilded. The statue is hollow from within. It portrays Buddha Sakyamuni in the posture of meditation; the position of his hand expresses mercy and warding off fear. His eyes are only open to a slit in his finely cut face, with wavy hair; the bump *(usnisa)* is missing from the top of his head. His slim body is half naked to the waist. The proportions of the body and the hair-style are rather typical of a Bodhisattva.

74 (a-b) **Genji Album.** Tosa School.
17th century
Coloured miniature paintings on paper with golden ornamentation
Height: 22 × 24.5 cm per table
Narrative scroll pictures and picture albums use the tale of Genji, this famous work by Lady Murasaki which dates from the eleventh century as one of their most frequent subjects. The first horizontal scroll picture to depict episodes from the tale dates from the mid-twelfth century and was made in the style of the Jamato School.

The Jamato School presented scenes of daily life in a typically Japanese, decorative style. The Tosa School carried on these traditions and between the sixteenth and nineteenth centuries produced many ornately bound picture albums, mainly intended for women.

The 54 miniatures in this album depict scenes from the 54 chapters of the novel. The episodes unfold from a richly gilded cloudy background. The lively colours are dominated by green. The rooms can be looked into from above, in the traditional bird's-eye view perspective. The faces of the static figures are indicated by a few lines, and the pictures concentrate on the decorative patches of splendid garments, coloured curtains and screens.

75 CHI PAY-SHI (1862–1957):
Bamboo
Size of the picture: 74.7 × 34 cm
Size of the whole scroll: 208 × 46.5 cm
Painted on paper with black India ink and mounted on a vertical scroll with a silk brocade frame, the picture is the work of the greatest twentieth-century Chinese painter, of whose virtually countless pictures twelve are preserved in the Museum. He employed the style known as "idea writing" with its bold calligraphic lines, making use of the play of the imperfect imprint of the half-dry brush, known as the „dry brush" technique. The signature and stamp of the painter appear in the lower left corner of the work, which dates from the late 1920s or the early '30s.

76 CHI PAY-SHI (1862–1957):
Autumn Fragrance, Autumn Hue.
1948
Painted on paper with India ink and in colours. (A form of *kakemono*, i.e. a picture mounted on a hanging scroll, with a silk brocade frame.)
The large patch of India ink represents a rock whose blackness contrasts well with the red of the haning spray of flowers that sprouts from beneath it.

The four large ideograms on the left-hand side of the picture, which express the title of the work in Chinese characters, have been written in archaic calligraphy; the text in cursive script underneath reads, "Old man Chi Pay-shi, 88 years"; below that is the red imprint of the artist's seal.

Chi Pay-shi was also noted as a calligrapher. He always carved his seals for himself.

77 LANG SHI-NING (1698–1768):
White Monkey
Size of the picture: 99.5 × 47 cm
Size of the whole scroll: 230 × 63 cm
The Italian missionary and painter, originally called Giuseppe Castiglione, spent the major part of his life in China as a court painter, where he mastered the technique and style of Chinese painting. This scroll picture, meant for suspension, is in water-colour on silk and mounted on paper. It depicts in minute detail the hero of a Chinese tale, White Monkey, set against the typical blank background of Chinese pictures. The name of the painter appears in the lower left corner of the picture. The four red stamps betoken the original owner, the Emperor Chien-lung.

78 (a) Cloisonné Enamel Vase.
Mid-15th century
Height: 17.3 cm, diameter of base: 7.6 cm, diameter of mouth: 4.3 cm
The vase is one of the earliest pieces of the collection representing *cloisonné* enamel work, which spread in China from the fourteenth century onwards. It dates from the golden age of the art of *cloisonné* enamel in the Ming period; with a typically thick enamel layer and uneven surface. The base is of brass with sparse gilding. The predominant colour is turquise blue; the lotuses covering the body of the vase and the trilobate leaves and five-petalled flowers decorating its neck are in green, red, yellow, blue and white.

(b) Cloisonné Enamel Wall Vase.
18th century
Height: 15.8 cm, width: 10.5 cm
The vase is intended to be suspended on the wall and so its back is flat and unornamented. It represents the archaizing art of the eighteenth century, with lustreless enamelling, an intentionally rough surface and strictly symmetrical ornaments symbolizing good luck and good wishes. The jade plate set in the middle of the vase has a poem by the monarch of the time, Emperor Chien-lung, engraved in it. The predominant colours of the enamel ornament are turquoise blue and pale green, with certain motifs in red and yellow enamel. The jade plate is black with a small white spot.

79 (a) Comb with Case. 17th century
Height: 6 cm, length: 13 cm
The lobate gold case of the Malayan horn comb is decorated with gold filigree foliated flowers. The red colour of the gold background and the yellow of the gold filigree had been achieved with different chemical processes. The ornament is one of the widely spread basic decorations,

which was used both in wood-carving and goldsmithery.

79 (b) Sword Hilt. 17th century
Height: 11.8 cm, diameter: 5 cm
The hilt, with the sword that belonged to it, was part of the insignia of a Malaysian ruler, worn at his inauguration.

The hilt is of cylindrical wood, somewhat flaring out upwards and covered with regular, dense leather-like carving. The gold-plated rings at the top and the bottom are decorated with rosettes, the upper rosette set with rubies. The front has a large, stylized gold leaf ornament set with diamonds and rubies, the back is decorated with two small triangular pieces of gold plates, inlaid with rubies, linked to the ring.

80 Book Plate. St Gallen. *c.* 900
Ivory, flat carving, 23.5 × 10 cm
A number of arts, including ivory carving, were for a long time dominated by Byzantine style. In the second half of the tenth century, the effect of antique, German, Italian and Byzantine influences led to a new style in bone-carving, which had its centre in the Rhineland.

This carved bone plate, held by some to be a book plate, is a typical example of that style. The rectangular plate is divided into two fields, the upper field showing Christ on the cross flanked by two saints, in a frame of Romanesque style foliage ornament. In the lower field is a turreted building between two trees, with the figures of two warriors.

To the left an angel sits on a building, and to the right two female figures with censers. The companion piece of this plate, the back part of the one-time cover, is in the Germanisches Nationalmuseum in Nuremberg. The plate has been transferred to the Museum of Applied Arts from the National Museum.

81 Book Cover. Transylvania. 1629
Light brown gilded leather, 31.7 × 20.4 cm
The picture shows the front and the spine of the richly gilded leather cover. According to its inscription, the volume entitled *Feidelmecnek serkentő oraia* (Stimulating Hour for Princes), published in Bártfa

(now Bardejov, Czechoslovakia) in 1628, was owned by Catherina of Brandenburg, the wife of Prince Gábor Bethlen of Transylvania. The ornament on the cover is a local variant of the so-called *à la fanfare* pattern of Western origin: a braided arrangement with flower stems and tendrils, ornamented with tiny sirens, fauns and birds. It was presumably the work of a Transylvanian bookbinder, testifying to the high standard of culture in Transylvania at the time.

82 Tapestry (the "Győr Tapestry").
Brussels, *c.* 1520
Coloured wool, woven of silk and gold threads, 275 × 260 cm
First mention of this tapestry in Hungary was made in 1601, when it was in the possession of Demeter Napragi, Bishop of Győr, who in 1619 bequeathed it to Győr Cathedral. The design of the tapestry is ascribed to Philippe de Bruxelles, and the work of weaving to the workshop of Pieter van Aelst. It was purchased by the Emperor and King Francis Joseph I, who presented it to the Society of Museum Friends for the Museum of Applied Arts.

The tapestry presents the adoration of the child Jesus. The Holy Family are surrounded by a group of angels and shepherds praying and playing on antique instruments. The two sibyls on the two sides hold a banderole with an inscription. In keeping with medieval tradition, the tapestry displays the events of the Nativity in several scenes within the same picture. A tapestry with the same subject and design is preserved in the Seminary Museum of Trento, as a part of the series "The Life of Jesus". The tapestry in the picture presumably formed part of a series too.

83 Chasuble. Hungarian embroidery on Venetian velvet. Early 16th century
Patterned velvet brocade; the cross embroidered in gold and silk
Length: 101 cm
The material of the chasuble is red velvet brocade interlaced with gold, in a pattern of Renaissance pomegranate motifs. In the longitudinal limb of the embroidered cross are the Virgin and Child under a domed

canopy supported by columns, with the figures of the Hungarian saints of St Stephen and St Ladislas below them. Right and left to the Blessed Virgin are the half figures of St Hieronymus and St Augustine. Hungarian saints often feature in embroideries with Hungarian objects.

84 Rug (so-called "Transylvanian rug"). Usak (Anatolia, Asia Minor). 17th century ·Knotted of coloured wool; number of knots: 1292/sq.dm. 168 × 121 cm

As early as the fifteenth century, splendid rugs were made in the town of Usak in Asia Minor. In the seventeenth century, the popular Usak rugs were purchased by Transylvanian tradesmen, through whom they reached Western Europe—hence the attribute "Transylvanian".

The Usak rugs, including the one in the picture, have a well-arranged pattern, with velvety shining bristles and the number of knots varying between 1,100 and 2,000 per sq.dm. Characteristic features of the pattern are the double *mihrab* (prayer niche) and the flower and tendril decoration in the border. The dominating colours are red, blue and yellow. Their pattern developed under Persian influence, while the ornaments of flowers and tendrils show Turkish influence. Most of the Greek inhabitants of the town of Usak were carpet-weavers, and they also left their mark on the rugs. This popular type of carpet often features in the pictures of old masters as an element of background decoration or to characterize the environment.

85 Table-cloth. Upper Hungary (now Czechoslovakia). 17th century
Linen cloth with blue cotton woven pattern, 180 × 71 cm

The ornate woven pattern of the cloth is akin to the fustian *(boccaccino)* black-cloth weaving, a technique dating from the thirteenth century and originating in Tuscany, which was developed under the influence of the Lucca silk weaving. Similar cloths were made in several countries of Europe, including Northern Hungary, where King Sigismund had fustian weavers settled in some major towns in the fifteenth century.

They formed their own guild at Kassa (now Košice, Czechoslovakia). The cloth was much sought after and even imported. This table-cloth differs from fustian cloth in its special plain weave.

The stripes of the characteristic pattern are reminiscent of the Saracen fabrics of Sicily. In the sixteenth and seventeenth centuries, the original geometrical patterns were slowly replaced by elements taken from nature: the motif of the tree of life with animal figures facing each other on both sides. Human figures and inscriptions in Gothic letters also occur. In this cloth the older and newer elements appear together. This store of motifs was to influence folk art for several centuries.

86 The Holy Family
Boxwood carving; German, 1500–50
17 × 17.4 × 13 cm

Boxwood with its fine fibrous substance and hard wood was used in wood-carving from early times, mainly for statuettes. It played a major role in Europe in the Middle Ages and the following centuries, and is used even today in China and the East Indies for figurines with many delicate details, objects for everyday use and ornamental pieces.

This sculptural group, with the expressive features of the figures, their natural gestures, the presentation of draperies and the atmosphere of the work as a whole, reflects the style of German Renaissance carving. Its humanistic content recalls the great German Renaissance masters.

87 St John
Boxwood carving; Flemish, *c.* 1500
Height: 18 cm

This statue, carved with delicate care, makes use of all the possibilities inherent in boxwood. Its value is enhanced by the fact that it came to the Museum of Applied Arts from the György Ráth collection. The gesture of the standing figure, the hands clutching the robe and the grief reflected in the noble features, offer an overwhelming presentation of inner life.

The statue was presumably part of a Calvary group.

88 Icon

Cretan–Venetian circle, 17th century
Painted on a panel against a gilded background, 80 × 60 cm

Icons, the panel paintings of the Eastern Orthodox Church, represented, under Byzantine influence in the Middle Ages, rigid compositions of saints with grave expressions. Although they expressed majesty and sincere devotion, by adhering to strictly set rules, they had an impeding effect on artistic development. Later the situation changed. The most eminent representative of the new, more unrestricted and human manner of representation was Andrei Rublev in the fifteenth century, who broke with rigid conventions and made his depictions approximate to real life. He had a profound influence on the icons of the following centuries. This icon already presents a meek and gentle Blessed Virgin, set free from conventions and radiating human emotions. The lively and lighter colours bring her even closer to the spectator. The painter maintained the usual gold background; this and the Greek inscription in the open book in the Child's hand still reflect Byzantine influence, but the throne decorated with acanthus leaves and the gentle look of the figures already link the representation to the approaching Renaissance.

89 Goblet with Cover

(the so-called Szapolyai Goblet), Nuremberg, c. 1520, signed
A chrysoprase bowl in a hammered, cast, engraved silver gilt mounting
Height: 56 cm

The foot and stem of the goblet and the handle of the cover imitate the ground, a gnarled trunk and a fruit-bearing branch, all ornamented, together with the blown cover, with little flowers and animals. The bowl is of chrysoprase (a pale green variety of chalcedony, a semi-precious stone also occurring in Transylvania). The goldsmith's signature on the cover and the foot has not been elucidated, and may be read as any of the letters p, n or o. The coat of arms incised on the cover has been identified by Jenő Radisics with that of János Szapolyai's, hence the name of the goblet.

According to Elemér Kőszeghy, the chrysoprase came from Transylvania, and it might have been processed in Buda at the end of the fifteenth century. The mounting is of a later date. The extraordinarily delicate details of the object deserve special attention.

90 Triton and Amphitrite. Pendant.

Italian or German work, c. 1600
Gold, with enamel, jewels and pearls, 9.5 × 7.3 cm

This kind of pendant (jewellery suspended from a necklace) was particularly popular in the sixteenth to eighteenth centuries. They often represented definite themes, frequently from Greek and Roman mythology, also using figurines in the round attached to the pendant, mostly decorated with *ronde bosse* enamel technique (the surface of the figures covered with enamel layers in different colours).

This pendant, coming from the treasury of Prince Esterházy of Fraknó (now Forchtenstein, Austria) was made of 22-carat gold, decorated with various enamels, diamonds, rubies and pearls. Besides the beauty of the valuable materials the decorative, solemn splendour of the jewel is also worthy of attention.

91 Amor's Ship

Pendant. German work, 17th century
Gold with *champlevé* and *ronde bosse* enamel, rubies and diamonds
Height: 10 cm

These ornate jewels often represented religious themes and also mythological and mundane symbols, mainly those referring to love. The depictions of ships of Italian origin often used irregular, so-called Baroque pearls. This pendant depicts a ship of mother-of-pearl shell, with a heart pierced with an arrow on the sail. There are several little coloured figures in *ronde bosse* enamel on the ship; the figure of Amor shooting his arrow once stood in the prow, but is now missing. These finely executed pendants were meant to enhance female beauty and aristocratic pomp.

92 Jug. German (Kreussen). 17th century

Stoneware with protuberant ornamenta-

tion, a pewter lid and oil enamel painting
Height: 18 cm
Stoneware, made of quartzose clay which becomes very hard and solid when baked at high temperature, was a favourite material for vessels in the German-speaking regions in the sixteenth to eighteenth centuries. They are often typified by protuberant ornaments and a pleasant harmony of pale colours. The material was often used for cups, jugs and beer-mugs. It thrived between 1560 and 1610, with Siegburg, Raeren and Kreussen as its centres.

This jug has a protuberant band running round its belly, depicting the twelve apostles with their names in coloured painting. The date 1673 appears under the handle. The beauty of stoneware jugs was rediscovered by nineteenth-century Historism, and they were copied in large numbers.

93 Mantelpiece Clock
Paris, early 19th century
Gilded bronze on marble pedestal
Height: 54.5 cm
Bronze is one of the oldest known metals. It was for a long time used in many different ways in Europe and in the East.

Bronze sculpture gained great importance during the Renaissance period in Europe, mainly in Italy and Germany.

In France, bronze sculpture flourished during the reign of Louis XIV, when it also played a major role in applied arts, being used for splendid gilded bronze clocks, candelabra and frames.

Under the reign of the Emperor Napoleon I, gilded bronze craft saw a revival within the formal realm of Neo-Classicism. Tastes turned towards antiquity, and Empire became a widespread style. This is also apparent in the choice of subjects, with a preference for ancient and Egyptian figures and ornaments.

This clock, with its grey marble pedestal and the classical statue of the winged genius, was meant to be placed on a mantelpiece or a commode, to create a grave and solemn atmosphere.

The body of the clock is decorated with a palmette motif with medallions, and the pedestal with gilded bronze studs, in the spirit of Neo-Classical art.

52

94 Haban Dish, with I S initials, Northern Hungary, with the date 1695
White tin-glazed faience, painted with metallic oxide paints (copper, chrome, cobalt, manganese)
Diameter: 31.5 cm
The Anabaptist Habans were persecuted in many countries of Europe, forcing them to set out as wanderers. Their first group settled in Hungary around 1530, and cultivated several trades, including faience craft, on a high level, in their specific, secluded "Haushabens". Their works showed several influences, including, from the 1670s onwards, that of Delft ware, which is also evident in this dish.

The dish has all the characteristic features of seventeenth-century Haban faience plates: the bowl becomes wider and shallower, the rim narrower. Also typical are the crowded presentation of late Renaissance flower motifs, the solid five-petalled rosettes and the dominance of the blue colour. The dish shows kinship with the so-called Máriássy-Berzeviczy dish, which bears the date 1695, and that refers to a Haban workshop in Northern Hungary. The date and the Jesuit emblem on the rim seem to indicate that it was made for a Jesuit monastery in Northern Hungary. The activity of the Habans marked an important chapter in the history of Hungarian ceramics.

95 Honeycake Mould, with M S initials and the date 1631. Provenance: Kassa (now Košice, Czechoslovakia)
Walnut, with hollowed-out carving
Diameter: 54 cm
The custom of shaping pastes into symbolic forms reaches back to ancient times. Honeycake was moulded in carved, wooden moulds, often of artistic quality, as early as the Middle Ages, but mainly in the sixteenth to eighteenth centuries. The Museum has acquired lovely carved moulds from the collections of Ágoston Szalay.

This mould depicts the Holy Trinity, surrounded by twelve apostles, in its frame. It shows the influence of South German Baroque carving.

As several similar moulds with the initials M S and I S have been found in

Northern Hungary, this specimen is thought to have come from the workshop of a family of carvers in Northern Hungary.

96 ANTOINE CRIAERD:
Commode. *c.* 1740
With rosewood veneer, palisander marquetry and bronze studs
86 × 145 × 56 cm
In the seventeenth to nineteenth centuries French furniture-making became a model for artistic style, taste and craftsmanship all over Europe.

The Museum of Applied Arts systematically collects fine pieces of French furniture and has acquired many specimens signed by notable masters.

This Rococo chest of three drawers, with its rosewood veneer, fine palisander marquetry, gilded bronze studs and artistic design is among the finest pieces of cabinet-making *(ébénisterie)*.

97 L. C. TIFFANY
(b. 1848, New York–d. 1933, New York):
Vase and Goblet. *c.* 1900
Polychromatic iridescent and opalesque glass
Height of vase: 35 cm, height of goblet: 22.3 cm
At the end of the nineteenth century a new artistic movement started in Britain. Breaking away from all which had gone before and drawing upon nature, it wished to express the emotional realm of the man of the period, and with its novel outlook created new models of beauty. Art Nouveau spread rapidly both in Europe and overseas.

Louis Comfort Tiffany founded the Glass and Decorating Company in New York in 1879. His new forms and the extremely impressive colour and light effects scored great successes at the World Exhibitions in Paris in 1900 and in St Louis in 1904. A typical feature of his pieces is their iridescent, opalesque light. The technique called *favrile*, glass lustred with gold, is one of his favourite solutions.

98 JÓZSEF RIPPL-RÓNAI
(b. 1881, Kaposvár–d., 1927, Kaposvár):
Woman in Red. 1898
Embroidered wall hanging, 230 × 125 cm
The painter József Rippl-Rónai also made valuable works in several genres of applied art. He designed ceramics, glass, tapestry and embroideries. He drew the inspiration for it from his relationship with artists during his stay in Paris. He deliberately turned to arts and crafts, mainly objects for everyday use, as he identified himself with the judgement of the day according to which art should be made available for everyone, and human life made valuable and accomplished by improving the environment and the objects in daily use.

This wall hanging, a typical *fin-de-siècle* work, was made for the dining-room of Count Tivadar Andrássy. The blue-grey linen material is completely covered with embroidery in coloured wool thread, using satin stitch—the work of the painter's wife, Lazarine.

99 Pharmacy Furniture (detail). 1744
Made in the Kőszeg joiner's shop of the Jesuits, under the foreman József Codelli Oak, in places with walnut veneer and carved details, for a room of 690 × 510 cm.
Displayed in the Kőszeg Pharmacy Museum
Designed for a vaulted room, built in all around, with doorways at the two sides and in the middle. Over the bench with opening seat which runs round the walls, is a section of curved drawers, with the open shelves above them ending in a cornice which follows the line of the vaulting. The glass-case cupboards in the two corners can be shut; in the middle stands a table with drawers. The paintings over the doors: Madonna with Child, SS Cosmas and Damian, are works by one "Dominus Etl". Some more recent additions include a painting entitled *Hungarian King*, a clock, wooden statues of standing Negro figures, and faience and wooden medicine pots of various provenances. The ensemble is one of the most important Hungarian Baroque interiors.

Ethnographical Museum

Like several other museums in Hungary, the Ethnographical Museum grew out of the National Museum. It was originally set up as the Ethnographical Department of the National Museum, with its material coming from earlier collections, particularly objects collected by János Xántus in the Far East. Ethnography itself was just emerging, rising step by step to the rank of an independent discipline.

Of the collections of the Museum those comprising universal ethnography became enlarged at a faster pace than the Hungarian ones. Among the first acquisitions were Antal Reguly's collection, small in number but of high scholarly value, which he brought home from his tour of Russia in 1845, studying the peoples of Finno-Ugrian languages living in that country, and presented to the Academy of Sciences in 1847. The Ob-Ugrian arrows from the first half of the nineteenth century and the embroidered chemises from the Ob-Ugrians and the Volga region are of unique value as a source for scholarly research.

From the start the collecting activity of the Museum covered all peoples of the world, including the peoples of the Carpathian Basin and those living in pre-First World War Hungary. At the turn of the century, the collections from Hungary still lagged behind those of universal ethnography. The decades after the establishment of the Museum determined the tasks and trends of the work of collecting and the objectives of research.

The first director, János Xántus, advocated the work of collection, preservation and display. From 1893 onwards, his successor, János Jankó, added scholarly processing to the activity of the Museum, which thus became able to perform all the functions of a museum.

Without aiming at completeness, some of the internationally outstanding collections deserve special mention. The nineteenth century saw the awakening of interest in the nature peoples, for a long time given the attribute "primitive". Research workers of the rich colonial countries with maritime navigation, were of course in a more favourable position in their research and collecting work. The collections of the Ethnographical Museum were set up under less favourable conditions, in the late nineteenth century. In 1896, Lajos Bíró went to the South Sea Islands as an entomologist, and spent six years in New Guinea and other islands. He soon extended his research work to other fields, and enriched the Museums with some 3,500 objects, and with unique notes and photographs.

Sámuel Fenichel's study tour to Oceania about the same time yielded a considerable enlargement for the Museum in other fields. The two initiatives were complemented by the activity of Rudolf Festetics, who expanded the region of Oceania represented in the collection.

Emil Torday and Sámuel Teleky brought valuable collections from East Africa. Between the two world wars the material was further enlarged with Rudolf Fuszek's collection from Liberia. The aboriginal culture of Australia reached the Museum through the collecting work of Géza Róheim.

By the end of the nineteenth century research into Hungarian prehistory came to the fore, mainly encouraged by the preparations for the millenary celebrations, i.e. the 1000th anniversary of the Hungarian Conquest, and made itself felt in ethnography too. There was a growing interest in the cognate peoples. In 1889, Károly Pápai added several hundred Ob-Ugrian objects (from North-west Siberia) to the Reguly collection. In 1898, János Jankó brought home hundreds of Ostyak, Cheremissian, Mordvinian and Votyak objects. Also in those years, Béla Vikár set the foundations of a Finnish and Aladár Bán of an Estonian collection. In 1912 Benedek Baráthosi Balogh presented a large Zyryan and Yurak-Samoyedic (Nenets) collection. The culture of the nomadic animal-keeping peoples of Central Asia is represented mainly by objects from György Almássy's collection. All that material formed the foundations of later collections. The Finnish collection, for example, has been enlarged on several occasions, while the material culture of the Bulgarian-Turkish peoples is represented by Gyula Mészáros's Bashkir and Chuvash collection. After the untimely death of János Jankó in 1902, there was a slackening in the enlargement of the universal ehtnographic collections, but it was still continued until the First World War.

Together with the Finnish and Estonian material mentioned already, the peoples of Europe were mainly represented by the Balkan peoples, the Lapps and the Austrians. Other regions of Europe unfortunately did not come into the focus of interest.

Only after the Second World War could collecting work be extended both geographically and thematically, first of all through exchanges. The Asian collection established by János Xántus, for instance, was enlarged by Benedek Baráthosi Balogh's collection among the Manchurian–Tungusian peoples of the Amur region, the Caucasian collection of the Zichy expedition, and several purchases (e.g. of Tibetan, Indian, etc. materials).

After the Second World War, Vilmos Diószegi's research work on Shamanism enriched the Museum with Siberian and Mongolian shaman requisites of outstanding value. The traditional culture and archaic civilizations of the peoples of the New World are represented mainly by objects from Mexico and South America, typical collections of Greenland and Alaska Eskimoes, and objects collected during a post-war expedition in Brazil and Venezuela, representing aboriginal Indian cultures.

The work of research and processing gained new impetus in Hungarian ethnography in the second half of the nineteenth century. The foundation of the Ethnographical Society of Hungary (today called Hungarian Ethnographical Society) in 1889, and the launching of its periodical, *Ethnographia,* in the following year, marked major stages in the history of ethnography. The first volumes of *Ethnographia* included articles on the Ethnographical Museum's collections, and the Society not merely urged collection work, but also outlined future tasks.

The study of the peoples living beyond Hungary's borders has been increasingly supplemented with the collection of material within the country's borders. The trend of the work was essentially determined by the approach of the millenary celebrations and the rediscovery of folk art. During the first years of the existence of the Ethnographical Society and its periodical, preparations were already going on for the celebration of the millenary of the Hungarian Conquest, and the goals of the various disciplines, permeated with the spirit of national movements, were closely linked to that event. Prior to that, János Xántus mainly urged the collection of handicraft tools and products, with a rather broad interpretation of the concept of handicrafts. That endeavour brought forth the collection of ceramics, costumes and furniture, and gave an impulse to the collection of Hungarian artefacts.

The experiences gained at the Vienna World Exhibition and the prevailing trends in applied arts directed attention to peasant and provincial culture. It is small wonder that aesthetic requirements often overshadowed other considerations, romantic views prevailed, and the collectors often looked for exoticism during their researches in Hungary. All that was further enhanced by the millenary celebrations, so much so that for a long time there prevailed an idyllic picture about the peasant way of life, considering its phenomena as an ancient legacy. Nevertheless, the period saw the setting up of valuable ethnographical collections, and the material of the Museum was growing at an unprecedented rate.

Despite the millenary attitude, the new material as a whole is not characterized by the prevalence of aesthetic requirements.

The work of Ottó Herman had a decisive influence on the research work of the time. His scientific and historical approach differed from the concept just outlined. He aimed at becoming acquainted with complete modes of life and collecting their material documents, as for example of fishing and the work of the shepherd. His results featured in the scientific and cultural programmes of the millenary celebrations in a separate collection.

Hungarian ethnographical research work, including the collection of relics, which emerged in the late nineteenth century, also covered the cultures of the various nationalities living in the country's territory at the time. Even the statutes of the Hungarian Ethnographical Society included research work among the national minorities living in the country as a task to be performed. The publications in *Ethnographia* and the collections of the Museum bear out the realization of this outlook in daily practice.

Jankó, who was well versed in the scholarly aims and methods of the time and excelled in the work of collection, processing and interpretation, set the trend of the Museum's development. While working on regional monographs, he took an active part in the organization of the preparations for the Millenary Exhibition, the collection and presentation of its material, and he also supervised the ethnographical work of the museums in the country. It may be safely said that the use of comparative research is linked with his name in Hungarian ethnography. With his work *A magyar halászat eredete* (The Origin of Hungarian Fishing), he also demonstrated that ethnography is a historical science, with a role in the research of Hungarian prehistory as well.

The ethnographical material of the Millenary Exhibition was later handed over to the Ethnographical Museum. The collection consisted of reconstructions of 25 peasant houses from various regions of the country, of an uneven scholarly value but still of major significance, as it contained complete interiors. The Museum had previously attempted to assemble interiors for two exhibitions abroad (in Paris and Vienna), which brought international acknowledgement, but the comprehensive character of the millenary material was until then unparalleled in Hungary. Part of the material collected by Ottó Herman on fishing and the keeping of sheep, was also presented to the Museum. In 1902, at the death of Jankó, the Museum possessed 37,000 objects, which means that within ten years the stock of its collections increased by 31,000 items. New additions included a collection of photographs and Béla Vikár's phonograph cylinder collection of folk music. Research work was assisted by the well-arranged, high-quality library. The picture would be incomplete without mentioning that Jankó also launched the Museum's journal, the *Néprajzi Értesítő* (Ethnographical Bulletin), and started the publication of catalogues of the material as part of the series "The Hungarian National Museum's Ethnographical Collections". Driven by the need to direct the work of collection and processing in the Museum, he embarked on arranging the main types of the Hungarian material in a *catalogué raisonné*, but he could only make the preparations for the work, which was finally edited and published by Zsigmond Bátky, under the title *Útmutató néprajzi múzeumok szervezésére* (A Guide to Organizing Ethnographical Museums).

The last two decades of the nineteenth century brought a lively interest in folk art, which also left its mark on the line of development of the collections, giving way to aesthetic considerations and requirements.

By the end of the nineteenth century, in the course of barely thirty years, the Ethnographical Museum developed into a major institution on an international scale. Its consolidation, collections and research work made it the leading and for a long time the sole notable institution of Hungarian ethnography. This explains the fact that unlike other similar institutions, its research and collection were not limited to the material relics of folk culture but included intellectual relics with similar enthusiasm.

The work of collecting folk music, initiated by Béla Vikár, was continued by Béla Bartók, Zoltán Kodály and László Lajtha, and resulted in a peerless folk-music collection, which became the basis for Hungarian folk-music research.

After Jankó's death, the work he had planned and commenced was continued by his successors, his former co-workers, but with less energy and purposefulness than he had brought to it.

The new generation, usually linked with the names of Zsigmond Bátky, István Györffy and Károly Viski, began its activity after the First World War. The Museum outgrew its home in a tenement house in Csillag utca, and moved to the Industrial Exhibition Hall in City Park, and in 1924, to the building of a grammar school on Könyves Kálmán körút. In 1973 it obtained the wing previously occupied by the Hungarian National Gallery in the building which had once housed the Supreme Court, and began moving in during 1975.

Besides enlarging the Hungarian collections, the Museum seized every opportunity to enrich its universal ethnographical collections. This process was interrupted by the First World War. The rapidly dwindling financial resources brought a set-back in collection work. Fortunately the same did not apply to research and processing activities. The Museum's collections served as the basis for the largest enterprise in Hungarian ethnography between the two world wars, *A Magyarság Néprajza* (Ethnography of the Hungarian People) and even though the publication was not the Museum's undertaking, a whole range of chapters were written by members of its staff. But the grave financial conditions led to the discontinuance even of the journal *Néprajzi Értesítő* for ten years.

The first organizational changes were planned during the Hungarian Soviet Republic in 1919. Accordingly the whole organization of the National Museum, and within it that of the Ethnographical Museum, would have been transfromed. Reconstruction was actually started, but could not be carried through.

Despite all the difficulties, the period between the two world wars saw some major results in the Museum's collecting activity as well. The value of the objects acquired at the time exceeds that of the earlier material, as their documentation was more precise, exact and detailed. The main directives in the trend of development were to complement existing collections, engage in thematic research and organize supplementary collections. The meagre resources for purchases prompted the Museum to establish exchange relations.

Following foreign, mainly Scandinavian, examples, in the 1930s people from widely diverse social background were drawn into the work of collection. The Museum organized a collecting network by correspondence, sending out questionnaires to gather data for its scholarly processing activity. The collection of photographs, which was set up by János Jankó, grew to considerable proportions, as did the material processed in the archives. Also following Scandinavian examples, a Documentation Section was set up in 1939, to preserve and arrange manuscript materials and make them available for research work. The collection of the Hungarian section of Folklore Fellows also was assigned to the Documentation Section.

The Second World War almost completely cut off the already narrow possibilities for activity and development. The permanent exhibition had to be closed and dismantled, and the collections crated and taken to security. The material could be made available once again only in 1946.

The war caused grave damage in the museum building, and the collections also suffered minor losses. The school building, which even in 1924 was cramped and unsuitable for the Museum's purposes, became more and more confined, and as it was situated in the outskirts of the city, could count on no real public interest. The Museum was faced with the choice of either mounting its earlier exhibition and waiting for appropriate storage for the rest of the material, or resting content with a smaller exhibition and using most of the rooms available for storage. The Museum opted for the latter solution, and in 1946–47 the equipment of the new store-rooms began. In 1947 a restoration workshop was set up, which actually meant the beginning of expert conservation and restoration of ethnographical museum pieces in Hungary.

Until 1947 the Ethnographical Museum was functioning as one of the departments of the National Hungarian Historical Museum, which was established by the museum law issued in 1934, within the organization of the National Museum. In 1947, it was divided from the Historical Museum—as was the Museum of Applied Arts—and became an independent national museum. The organizational order which was worked out at the time has remained valid ever since, with some modifications. The organization was built on the collections: the Hungarian Department was set up with the task of continuing to collect Hungarian material, and carrying out research work within the country; the International Department was given the task of collecting and processing objects from Europe and overseas, and engaging in universal ethnographical research. The Documentation Section also became a department. A few years later the library became an independent department as well, as did the folk-music collection. An economic department was set up as well. The museum staff also expanded, parallel with the growing number of departments, with the aim of having the collections entrusted to professional research workers equally qualified in enlarging and processing the material.

As soon as circumstances permitted, the conditions for scholarly research work were also reorganized. The library was soon made available, and opportunities opened for collection work. The staff members joined in the collection of the intellectual and material relics of the 1848 Hungarian Revolution, and in migration studies. The latter work mainly yielded results in the research of the post-war settlements in Transdanubia of Székelys from Bukovina and Csángós from Moldavia. A team carried out explorations of monographic quality in Tiszaigar and displayed the results of their collecting work at an exhibition, also publishing a study on them.

The scholarly research work of the following years was carried out in teamwork led by the Academy of Sciences. Staff members of the Museum played a leading role in several teams and headed national research projects. Monographic aims came to the fore in the collection of objects: to seek and collect the material relics of a given village or region, or to acquire all the relevant tools and products of a given trade. The last thirty-five years brought a tremendous development in the material, in terms of both quality and quantity. The number of objects in the collections of ceramics and costumes has been doubled, and similarly important progress is evident in the collections of furniture and farming tools. The Documentation Section saw a rapid growth in the number of photographs and manuscripts, while the library has risen among the country's large specialized libraries.

The Museum has always felt it its duty to display its material for the public. The mounting of exhibitions has never been suspended even under straitened financial conditions, and a great many temporary shows have been organized both within the Museum and in other halls, including a number of exhibitions abroad. The work of exhibiting has once again become systematic since 1975, and the first permanent exhibition "From Primitive Societies to Civilizations" was opened in 1980. The presentation of the material has also been served by publications: the *Néprajzi Értesítő* founded in 1900, the series "Hungarian Folk Art" between the two world wars, and *Néprajzi Közlemények* (Ethnographical Proceedings), *Adattári Értesítő* (Documentation Bulletin) and volumes of *Index Ethnographicus* have been launched after the Second World War.

The organization of an open-air ethnographical museum in 1965 meant a considerable expansion of the Museum's field of activity. A new organizational unit was set up for the work, which involved other staff members as well. The Open-Air Ethnographical Museum in Szentendre became a separate institution in 1972, and in 1974 it became fully independent from the Museum. New tasks involved the administration of private collections placed as a deposit, the examination of objects intended to be taken out of the country, the issuing of export permits and the supervision of provincial museums.

Progress and the newly emerging tasks have called for another rearrangement in the organization of the Museum. Now the Collection Department deals with the collections, their enlargement and processing. It has two sections: European and universal ethnography. The Department of Stock Protection sees to the protection, registration and treatment of the objects. It is divided into a Registrar's, a Stock Keeper's and a Restorers' Group and a Photographic Studio. The Folk Music Section was merged with the Ethnological Data Collection. This Documentation Department also has been assigned—beyond handling its own collections—the responsibility of organizing voluntary collecting activity. The tasks of the Library and the Economic Department have remained unchanged. The new Department of Public Education is divided into Groups of Education, Exhibition Organization and Publicity, all in close co-operation with the other Departments.

During the 110 years of its existence, the Ethnographical Museum has grown into one of the largest institutions of its kind in Europe. The number of objects it contains amounts to more than 150,000, one-third of which comes from outside Hungarian-speaking regions. The collection of manuscripts amounts to nearly 2,000,000 folios, the number of photographs comes to 300,000 and the material includes some 80,000 metres of motion film. The Museum also preserves original folk-music recording and notations by Béla Vikár, Béla Bartók, Zoltán Kodály and László Lajtha. The library stock surpasses 100,000 volumes.

János Kodolányi

DESCRIPTION OF ILLUSTRATIONS

100 Fur Bag
Sosva region, North-west Siberia. Ostyak
Height: 78 cm, width: 63 cm
A wide-mouthed reindeer-skin bag, rounded off at the bottom. The back side is decorated with a combination of pieces of light and dark coloured fur and pieces of fur with the pelt turned outside. In the front the pattern is made up of dark and light fur pieces cut out in designs and framed with pelt bands. The patterns in the rectangles in the middle depict bears, and the outer ones pine-martens. The mouth can be tied up with straps.

101 Poison Cup
Congo. Bewongo. No date
Height: 18 cm, diameter of mouth: 5.9 cm
The dark brown wooden cup is of a human figure, with the orifice at the top of the head. Both hands of the figure are behind his back, resting against his bottom. The two horns on the head are curving backwards, the place of the eyes is taken by metal plates. The front and back of the body are covered with carvings imitating tattoo designs.

102 Shaman's Mantle
Ulan ul, Mongolia. Soiot
Height: 79.5 cm, length of sleeve from the collar: 64.5 cm
Made of blue linen cloth, of mantle cut, opening on the right, with reindeer-skin collar. The sleeves are bordered with red and white stripes, with a wide black band at the bottom of the mantle and with yellow and red stripes at the lower end. In the middle of the back there are leather strips; flat and cylindrical strips hang at the waist, the first to the left decorated with an applied disc and the one in the middle with a cross-shaped trimming.

103 Dance Mask. 19th century
Liberia
Brown wood painted black on the outside
A so-called helmet mask, carved in wood, representing a human face, which takes up a relatively small space as compared with the rest of the head. On the top there is a trefoil-shaped carving. The eyes and the mouth are scarcely indicated. There are four round holes under the chin. The hair is indicated by richly grooved patterns. A

bird and a crocodile are on either side of the head. A reed ring is attached with a string to the lower end of the mask.

104 Statue
Veracruz, Mexico
Height: 48.7 cm, width: 27 cm
The statue of reddish-brown clay represents the standing figure of a smiling man, holding a rattle in his left hand. The head-dress is ornamented with geometrical patterns. A copy of a clay model from the first to sixth centuries A.D.

105 Beehive. 19th century
Nőtincs, Nógrád County
Height: 64 cm, diameter of base: 32 cm
A tub grooved out of a piece of hollow limewood and covered with a linden board. The semicircular flight slot is cut into a protuberance on the side, with incised stylized decoration above it. The holes in the side serve for the sticks that hold the honeycomb.

106 Salt-cellar. 1891
Lengyeltóti, Somogy County
Height: 9.3 cm, length: 9.7 cm, width: 3.5 cm
An oval box of horn with wooden bottom and lid. The lid shows two ram heads back to back. The side and rim of the lid are decorated with carving of rickrack pattern. The waxed carving on the box shows a flower pattern on one side resembling tulips and branching off from a pot, and on the other the Hungarian coat of arms, with semi-rosettes at the ends.

107 Powder-horn. 18th century
Magyarszákos (now Sacoşul rom, Rumania)
Height: 18 cm
A two-branched powder-horn cut from antlers. The braches have bottoms fitted to them. Metal loops are fixed to either side of the mouth. It is ornamented with incised and carved geometrical patterns, with a nine-armed swastika in the middle. The stylized patterns around the mouth and on both branches, flanked by rickrack bands, are reminiscent of human figures. The space above the human figures, holding hands, on the branches is filled with dotted ornaments.

108 Scab-grease Holder. 1914
Trans-Tisza region
Height: 9.5 cm, diameter: 7.5 cm
A holder with lid carved from ox-horn. The lid is attached to the case with a serrated winged ironwork of punched ornamentation, decorated with two copper-stars. This fitting can be fixed with a hinged turnable bolt. The wooden bottom is fastened to the body with four nails. The horn is pressed into an octagonal shape and is decorated with a scratched pattern. At the top and the bottom are ribbons of diamond-shaped ornaments. One of the main fields has a coat of arms in a wreath, flanked by the letters T and S, and the other field on the opposite side represents a shepherd holding a huge crook, with a dog, the initials K J and date 1914 behind him. The two narrow sides each have a flower-tree with six branches in a pot, each branch carrying a flower and a leaf, and the seventh flower is forming the fitting.

109 Mirror-case. 1840
Magyargencs, Vas County
Length: 12.3 cm, width: 10.4 cm, height: 1.9 cm
A square flat box of hardwood, with pull-out lids on the top and the bottom, ornamented with incised and carved patterns and figures in red, black and green waxing. On one side stands a shepherd in ornate felt cloak, with a crook and a long-stemmed pipe; his dog and a lamb with a bell are before him, under an oak. The other side shows an outlaw dressed like the shepherd; he forces a soldier who has dropped his rifle to his knees. The outlaw has a pistol and a swine-herd's hatchet. The scene is framed on three sides with undulating lines and six-petalled red rosettes. The date 1840 can be read at one side among rosettes.

110 Razor Case. 19th century
Ormánság, Baranya County
Length: 22.8 cm, width: 8.2 cm, height: 4 cm
A box with lid of hardwood, with semicir-

cular ends. The lid turns on a wooden shaft fixed to one end, and is ornamented with circular carvings of brown incised floral compositions. The mirror attached to the lid opens with a hinge-joint. The sides are decorated with figures of owls and a wild boar, and the bottom shows a stag and the inscription EMLÉK (Souvenir).

111 Stove Tile
Alsópáhok, Zala County
Height: 20.5 cm, width: 20.5 cm
A square plate of green lead-glazed fired clay, made in plaster mould. The decoration consists of a bird perched on a flowerpot, holding a tulip with a relatively large flower-cup in its beak, with smaller sprays below and above it. In the lower left corner the letters Po and in the right corner the letters SA appear.

112 Mirror. 19th century
Hódmezővásárhely, Csongrád County
Pine
Length: 67 cm, width: 40 cm
The inside frame shows Biedermeier influence; the corner rosettes have been removed. Attached to this frame is an outside frame with Rococo stylistic marks, with openwork carvings on its relief surface, and painted in many colours.

113 Chair. 1837
Kóny, Győr-Sopron County
Walnut and oak
Height: 96 cm, length: 44 cm, width: 38 cm, height of seat: 51 cm
The seat is of a curved outline, the four grooved legs are fixed to it by straps. The violin-shaped back is also joined to the seat, and is filled with carvings: the incised band in the middle, the heart-shaped aperture and the three bunches of flowers placed one above the other are surrounded by a Baroque frame. The initials C I and the date 1837 are set among the flowers. The whole back is decorated with inserted stars.

114 Church Chest
Rozsonda (now Ruja, Rumania)
Length: 159 cm, width: 62 cm,
height: 110 cm

The chest is made from beech-wood. The front and the two sides each consist of three boards and the back of four boards. The board legs are cut out at the bottom. The lid is roof-shaped, the edge of its front board has two wedged incisions on both sides and a square incision in the middle for the padlock clamp. In the interior is a deep drawer on the left. The front is painted in yellowish, brownish and greenish colours with black outlines. On each of the legs is the figure of a man, with a globe in his hand, in a vaulted frame, and with a round medallion above. The upper and lower boards of the front have four round medallions of a similar size, in plaited ribbon frames. The medallions depict figures resembling a lion against a pale green and red background alternately, and a version of the scene of the assumption of Alexander the Great.

115 Chest. 19th century
Decs, Tolna County
Pine
Length: 113 cm, width: 65 cm,
height: 93 cm
A high, square chest with broad-bottomed legs, and framed with rims at the top and the bottom. On the two side-borders in the front are lathe-turned engaged columns without capitals on a tall base.

116 Drinking Vessel. 19th century
Magyarhegymeg (now Uhorské, Czechoslovakia)
Length: 13 cm, height: 7.2 cm,
diameter: 8 cm
A hemispherical vessel carved from hardwood; the handle resembles a disc and depicts a coiled-up snake, biting into the rim of the vessel. On the outside it is decorated with tulips and stylized floral patterns in flat carving in a 3 cm wide band. On one side are birds on the top of a pine tree. The pattern terminates both at the top and below in a lacy decoration reminiscent of leather work. The figure of a lizard, with its body widening from the middle of the vessel upwards, runs through the centre of the vessel, with its head lying on the snake which forms the handle. On the bottom there is a hare and a fox on either side of

the lizard. The lower part, divided by a lath, imitates a drawer. The side-wall has an iron handle fixed to it. In the interior is a drawer to the left and a secret drawer at the bottom. The chest is painted in black, and has in the front a new panel framed by a few incised patterns and each enclosing two carved tulips. The whole pattern is covered with a rich, minutely executed red, white, yellow and green floral design.

117 Dish. 1780
Great Hungarian Plain
Diameter: 60 cm, height: 16 cm, diameter of base: 24 cm
Thrown lead-glazed fired clay, with shallow hollow and the rim bending inwards like a frame. The ground colour is greenish white; the decoration is filled out with reddish brown, olive green and reddish yellow, with red-brown outlines. The bold pattern fills out the whole dish, both the hollow and the rim. It shows a flowery bush growing out of a two-handled green vase, with three large flowers resembling pomegranates, and two reclining stems, in a symmetrical design. The contours were drawn with an incised quill. It is surrounded below the rim by several rows of thin stripes, broken by thin green and yellow lines, and a lace pattern above it with short lines in the intervals. The dish is wired, and has in the bottom engraved attempts at a coat of arms with the double eagle.

118 Bonnet. 19th century
Laskó (now Lug, Yugoslavia)
Length: 24 cm, width: 16 cm
Black linen with white satin-stich and raised embroidery, and thick seam. The hemming is in chain-stitch and the inside of the plum pattern in herringbone stitch. The embroidery depicts a male crab.

119 Szűr (Felt Cloak). 1883
Somogy County
Length: 101 cm, length of sleeve: 28 cm
A szűr cloak of white felt, with red appliqué and coloured wool embroidery, and a large collar. An ornament of thin plaited straps is suspended from the neck.

120 Ködmön (Jacket). 19th century
Mezőkövesd, Borsod-Abaúj-Zemplén County
Length: 44 cm, length of sleeve: 50 cm
A sheepskin jacket with white, red and green leather appliqué work, with long white sheep fur on the inside. The neck and front are hemmed with black fur and adorned with embroidery. The colours are dominated by pale shades. The back and most of the upper part of the sleeves are decorated with embroidery. Two leather tassels are attached at the waist. The pattern of the embroidery shows roses used by furriers.

121 Big Jug. 1744
Vörösberény, Veszprém County
Height: 38 cm, diameter of mouth: 14 cm, diameter of bottom: 14.5 cm
Thrown lead-glazed fired clay. The glaze is pale green with some yellow glaze effused to accentuate the embossed decoration. The neck is encircled with a band of pressed finger-marks. In the front is a double eagle, holding a sword in each of its legs, with the date 1744 on its breast. An incised bird with a flower appears on the side. The inscription is also incised: *Anno domini 1744 V. B. Birák és Esküt Uramék korsai.* The handle has a knob. The jug belonged to village magistrates and counsellors.

122 Bottle. 1879
Tiszafüred, Szolnok County
Height: 28.5 cm, diameter of bottom: 9.5 cm, diameter of mouth: 3 cm. Stone.
An oval bottle with a round mouth. It was made in 1879 by Lajos Katona for Gergely Kovács, who appears on the back, sitting in a boat with a pipe in his mouth and an oar in his hand, and an ornate hat on his head. The mounted hussar on the front depicts the commissioner, Lajos Kováts. The inscription is incised and the secondary ornaments are made with incised quill. The hues used are green and brown glaze and red earth colour. The figures are incised and coloured, and colourless glaze has been poured over the whole surface. The ground colour is earth colour from Dúd.

Budapest Historical Museum

The Budapest Historical Museum collects, preserves and processes archaeological and historical material (life-style, industry, culture, general history) of the peoples who have lived in the territory of today's Greater Budapest, and of the capital itself.

The Museum's predecessor, the Budapest City Art Gallery, was founded in 1887. The first objects came from the excavations carried out at the sites of the Roman period in Budapest, including the Roman civilian settlement at Aquincum, and the first exhibition was opened in 1890 in the newly established Aquincum Museum.

The same years saw the beginning of the collection of material from the Modern Age. The first exhibition displaying the Museum's material of local history was mounted in 1899 in a building in the City Park; in 1941 it was moved to the Kiscell Museum in the former Schmidt mansion in Óbuda.

The medieval collection was founded in the 1920s. The first exhibition of medieval local history was mounted on the Fishermen's Bastion in the Castle District in 1932, and from 1945 onwards the collection has been housed in the former Town Hall in Buda. In 1968, the Budapest Historical Museum moved into Wing E of the former Royal Palace. But the Kiscell Museum, the Aquincum Museum and smaller on-the-spot displays in the Roman military camp, the Flórián tér bath and the Hercules villa in Meggyfa utca, continued to remain integral parts of the Museum, which is thus a national institution housed in several buildings.

A major scholarly and political assignment for the Museum has been the writing of the history of Budapest. The preparations for a monographic treatment of the history of the capital took more than ten years of historical research, drawing on various archives, contemporary memoirs and archaeological investigations. Following preparatory research work, the five volumes of the history of Budapest were completed between 1973 and 1980, edited and published by Akadémiai Kiadó. The publishing of the five volumes filled a long-felt gap; they cover several historical ages, as Budapest is one of the oldest settlements in Europe.

Volume I: The history of Budapest from prehistoric times to the end of the age of the Árpáds (in 1301). Edited by László Gerevich.

Volume II: The history of Budapest in the late Middle Ages and during the age of the Turkish occupation of Hungary (1301–1686). Edited by László Gerevich and Domokos Kosáry.

Volume III: The history of Budapest from the expulsion of the Turks till the March Revolution (1686–1848). Edited by Domokos Kosáry.

Volume IV: The history of Budapest from the March Revolution till the Aster Revolution (1848–1918). Edited by Károly Vörös.

Volume V: The history of Budapest from the period of the two revolutions till the country's liberation (1918–1945). Edited by the late Miklós Horváth.

The five volumes, on 3,289 pages with 1,705 illustrations and 17 maps, give a monographic summary of the history of Budapest from the earliest times until 1945.

Parallel to the monographic historical treatment of the peoples who have lived in the area of today's Greater Budapest and of the history of the capital is a permanent exhibition which occupies about 1,000 square metres on the first floor of Wing E of the former Royal Palace and represents "Two Millennia of Budapest".

The pictures in the exhibition start out from the episode when the Romans built a city at the site of today's Budapest, which within one century became the capital of the province of Pannonia. The exhibition makes use of the latest archaeological discoveries of the 1970s: the site and structure and the relics relating to the mode of life of the Roman military camp which was rediscovered and excavated at Óbuda.

The exhibition displays a great many original finds relating to the history and way of life of the peoples who lived on the site of today's Greater Budapest in the Migration Period, which also saw the Hungarian conquest of Transdanubia at the beginning of the tenth century. Many archaeological finds dating from the period have also been found in the territory of the capital. Rich archaeological finds survived from the first Hungarian settlers in what is today Óbuda, Pestlőrinc and Farkasrét. According to tradition handed down to us by a medieval chronicler whose real name is unknown (Anonymus), Prince Árpád had his summer quarters on Csepel Island, while his co-ruler, the sacral prince Kursan, settled down at Óbuda. The clans of the Megyer tribe lived along the roads leading to the crossing places on the Danube, both on the Buda and the Pest sides. From the second half of the tenth century onwards, the common people settled in Csepel, Csillaghegy and Óbuda. The site of Budapest regained its central role by the end of the Migration Period, with the appearance of the conquering Magyars.

A rich contemporary material demonstrates the process of settlement which began after the Conquest and led to the formation of Budapest, in the natural centre of the country, at the borderline between the Great Hungarian Plain and Transdanubia, along the great trade routes and Danube crossing places that had been in use from time immemorial. The exhibition uses contemporary objects of great value, maps drawn up on the basis of original documents and statistical data to present the history of Budapest from the time of the establishment of the Hungarian State to the country's Mongol Invasion, and from the founding of Buda till the Turkish occupation.

A further section of the exhibition displays the 145 years of the Turkish occupation. A number of genuine and reconstructed objects reflect the rapid social and economic changes, followed at a slower rate by the transformation of the townscape. At first the Turks moved into existing medieval buildings and transformed them to their own requirements, but later they built edifices of their own, which show the stylistic marks of Ottoman architecture. The Museum houses a highly valuable collection from the time of the Ottoman Empire, bearing out that both the products of the Balkan provinces and the famous Turkish faience ware of Asia Minor reached the bazaars in Buda and Pest. Finds include Persian pottery, Chinese porcelain, famous celadon glazed earthenware and ornate pedestalled bowls from the Balkans.

The next section of the exhibition demonstrates the period during which the city, which was nearly destroyed in the battles to achieve liberation from the Turkish occupation, developed into the country's capital. The first phase of development, between 1686 and 1790, marks the time of reconstruction, resettlement and the rise into an economic, administrative and intellectual centre. The upswing of goldsmithery, for instance, which produced objects to satisfy the population's demands for luxury, is richly represented in the exhibition.

By the end of the eighteenth century, Buda and Pest formed the country's administrative and main trade centre—and were the most populous settlements and became the leading city of Hungary. To rise further in rank and become the real capital of the country it had to achieve a leading role in the political and intellectual field as well. The development in this respect represents the main content of the history of the period from 1790 to 1848 as illustrated by the relevant rich collection in the Museum.

A number of original objects and artistic replicas recall the history of Buda and Pest at the time of the 1848–49 bourgeois Revolution and War of Independence, and the age of absolutism. Of particular interest are the original objects which demonstrate that despite the Habsburg oppression, the capital became more and more the centre of Hungarian culture and of the national movement fighting absolutism with increasingly open means.

The following part at the exhibition presents the history of the capital from the unification of Buda, Pest and Óbuda until the 1918 Revolution. During those decades Budapest developed into a capitalist metropolis, the only really large city in the country, a transformation expressed both in the city's expansion, the fast growth in the number of inhabitants, the changes in the townscape, the progress in the build-up of public utilities and the changing social structure: the appearance of the capitalist and working classes, the sharpening of class distinctions and the strengthening of the labour movement. As a result of many years of systematic collection, the exhibition displays documents of the period's political life, its industrial and cultural history and the history of customs, as well as the history of the capital's labour movement.

In presenting Budapest as the capital city of two revolutions (1848–49 and 1918–19), the exhibition intends to emphasize the main features of the revolutionary path of Hungarian society, underlining the events linked to Budapest. National and local events are naturally interrelated, and that is particularly true for the time of the two revolutions, when Budapest was not only the centre of the country's administration but of the revolutionary events as well. The exhibition shows many original documents and objects displayed for the first time, about the Hungarian Soviet Republic, when the exemplary perseverance of the workers in the capital vitalized the first Hungarian proletarian dictatorship for 133 days. As illustrated with original documents and photographs, the achievements of the urban policy in that salient period in the history of Budapest also contributed to the growth of socialist political science.

Special mention should be made of the Hungarian and foreign photographs that bear witness to the fact that the Hungarian Soviet Republic was overthrown by the superior numbers of the Entente Cordiale and Little Entente.

Contemporary objects, photographs and archival documents exhibit Budapest under the fascist Horthy regime, together with the progressive, left-wing tendencies which played a major part in the capital's cultural, artistic and political life. A number of objects and photographs recall the horrors of the reign of the Arrow-Cross terror at the closing stages of the Second World War.

The permanent exhibition concludes with pictures on the liberation of Budapest in 1945 and the recommencement of life after the war. Every four hours the visitors can watch colour and black-and-white video tape recordings on the various periods of the capital's history.

The other permanent exhibition, entitled "The Royal Palace and Gothic Sculptures of Medieval Buda", displays the remnants and relics of the medieval palace, in an area including the subterranean parts of the museum building and the courtyards.

Between 1948 and 1963, large-scale archaeological excavations were carried out in search of the remnants of the medieval royal palace which had disappeared long ago. After the conclusion of the excavations, by 1968, the medieval royal palace was reconstructed as an art monument and an exhibition was mounted to display the fourteenth to fifteenth century royal court and the way of life of the time.

In 1974, during further excavations in Buda Castle, Gothic statues and torsos of great importance from an art history viewpoint were dug up in the northern forecourt of the medieval palace. These sculptures have raised the Museum's medieval collection to one of the most important Gothic galleries in Europe. The finds are of outstanding importance not only for Hungarian art history but also from a European aspect, representing unique values. Therefore, following general international practice, the missing parts have not been supplemented by material resembling the original stone in colour or character.

65

The Gothic sculptures had doubtless been made to ornament the medieval Buda palace, in some connection with the building itself, and so they have been erected in the excavated and reconstructed rooms of the medieval palace where they fit harmoniously into the concept of the presentation of the medieval building. The architectural space of the medieval palace, which also houses the Historical Museum, provides the framework for displaying the material finds of the court culture that once developed among its walls. The correlated presentation of the museum pieces together with the parts of the building in their original places *(in situ)* thus enables the visitors to sense the historical, architectural and artistic relationships of this cultural complex.

The Gothic statues were buried nearly 600 years ago; now the group of the secular statues has been exhibited in the Gothic hall of knights and the statues of saints, in the Gothic chapel—the two most important and representative areas in the excavated medieval palace, which with their architectural design duly underline the artistic significance of the sculptures. Their dimensions and proportions fit easily into the architectural spacial proportions, without however losing their individuality.

The material of the mounting units for the sculptures have been selected to correspond with the requirements of the structure, forms and interior design. The red marble pedestals fit in with the panelling, and the platforms of metal units have a reserved and neutral effect, being in harmony with the overall keynote of the already existing exhibitions. In some parts of the hall of knights and the chapel, the dominant effect of the background had to be toned down so that the stone walls with their rough texture should not unfavourably influence the delicate modelling of the statues.

The Gothic hall of knights houses 21 secular statues and the Gothic chapel has nine Madonnas and saints. A glass-case in the entrance to the hall of knights displays nine heads of statues and two figured corbels.

Relics dating from Roman times (A.D. 19 to the beginning of the fourth century) are displayed in the Aquincum exhibition. The exhibition "Roman Life in Aquincum" in the local museum presents the period of Roman rule. The five rooms of the exhibition recall the history of the Roman conquest of Aquincum, the economic life in the Roman town and the way of life, culture, art and religion of the inhabitants. A recent addition to the material came from the rediscovery and excavation of the Roman military camp during the construction work of the new Óbuda housing estate.

The Roman organ reconstructed from original parts is a unique piece of the exhibition even by world standards; the organ is sometimes even used in concerts organized by the Museum.

Recent achievements include the excavation and presentation of the convent of the Poor Clares, a major architectural object often mentioned in historical sources, which was founded by Queen Elizabeth, the mother of King Louis the Great. In the Buda Castle District, a Dominican monastery has been excavated, one of the earliest buildings in the city founded in the mid-thirteenth century. The church of the monastery was constructed before the Church of Our Lady (today's Matthias Church), and it was built over the remnants of the chapel of a settlement dating from before the Mongol Invasion (1241–42). The excavated remnants of the Dominican building have been incorporated into the structure of the Budapest Hilton Hotel, in keeping with the principles applied to art monuments.

Collecting work forms an integral part of the Museum's activity involving historiography, archaeology and mounting of exhibitions.

A major part of the Museum's material consists of the 2,000 pieces in the collection of engravings, including representations of the city. The collection grew out from the Ennea Lafranconi engraving material, which was presented to the capital; by now it comprises all the notable depictions of the city since that time. The collection of drawings and prints is of a similar character; together with portrayals of the city, it contains portraits of persons who have played some role in the life of the capital and representations of events and

66

fashions. The collection of nearly 65,000 paintings, sculptures, drawings and coins comprises works linked with the history of Budapest either through the events and sites depicted or the origin of the artist.

A rich collection displays objects related to the life and activity of guilds: guild-chests, sign-boards, guild badges, objects of daily use and ornamental pieces. There are valuable relics of viniculture in Óbuda: wine-presses and other relevant objects, and tools and objects of other trades that played major roles in the history of the capital: coach-craft, rope-makers, coopers and printers. Side by side with these collections are relics directly linked with the capital's history, such as objects that once belonged to the town councils, town halls and various corporations.

A major group includes relics of industrial history, mainly machines, machine parts and documents. In that field the Museum collects primarily relics which besides their technical significance also had a social effect on the capital's life, such as the Mechwart roller-frame, the first Déri–Bláthy–Zipernowszky transformer and the Csonka carburettor.

The documents consist of collections of photographs, films, maps, designs, manuscripts and prints. More than 50,000 photographs show events in the city's life, its buildings and personalities who played some role in its history. Particularly valuable is the complete collection of the photographer György Klösz from the nineteenth century. The Museum constantly enlarges its collection of photographs by taking pictures in a methodical and systematic manner of all the changes in the townscape (pulling down of buildings, new edifices, new features in town planning, etc.).

Besides its collection of photographs, the Museum also makes films about major events in the capital. It filmed, for example, the old Ganz foundry, now demolished, the reconstruction work at the royal castle in Buda and certain trades that are slowly dying out in Budapest. The maps and designs amount to several thousand items including plans of the Vigadó (Municipal Concert Hall), the Chain Bridge, the Tunnel, the Opera House, the Parliament building and the Fishermen's Bastion. Designs of city planning and urban development are of historical and economic significance, and the Museum has preserved such plans ever since the capital grew into a metropolis.

The collection of manuscripts and prints includes printed matter relating to city administration, bills, commemorative addresses, concert bills, programmes, playbills, pamphlets, posters and invitation cards, which help trace all the major events in the capital's history practically up to the present day.

The manuscripts include valuable items of Hungarian history and the cultural scene of the capital, for instance various documents of the 1848 Revolution, the minutes of the first meeting of the Committee of Public Noise Abatement, letters by Count István Széchenyi, the papers of the British architect Adam Clark, the builder of the Chain Bridge and the Tunnel, minutes of the National Council of 1918 and of the soldiers' and workers' council of the 1919 Hungarian Soviet Republic as well as the original manuscripts of Béla Bartók's *Dance Suite* and Zoltán Kodály's *Psalmus Hungaricus*.

Part of these collections is displayed at temporary exhibitions arranged according to subjects or genres in the Kiscell Museum.

The Memorial House of Béla Bartók, the outstanding figure in Hungarian and international music, also houses exhibitions of the Historical Museum. It is set up in Bartók's last Budapest home at No. 29 Csalán utca in the Second District, and the exhibits follow the composer's life story with the help of photographs, maps and material relics, presenting his *œuvre,* objects he himself collected, and his former study furnished with the original pieces of furniture. Recordings of his piano playing and various programmes also help popularize the work of the great composer. With its permanent Bartók exhibition and temporary displays, the Memorial House plays a major role in artistic education and developing musical tastes.

Together with its scholarly work, the Museum is also active in public education.

It maintains close contacts with school education. An educational team has been set up in the Museum, with the participation of history teachers in different types of school in Budapest. The team members discuss the forms and methods by which the exhibitions, objects and documents can be successfully incorporated into the curriculum. They give demonstration lessons for their colleagues, and organize programmes for students linked to the exhibitions. They participate in compiling comprehensive teaching aids, which also help them to talk about the contents of the Museum. A special class-room has been equipped with modern audio-visual devices for classes to be held in the Museum, and a special list has been drawn up of objects and materials selected from the Museum's collections and recommended for history teachers.

These objects are available for the students at the lessons held in the Museum's class-room, who can thus, through direct observation, better judge their function, material and technology, which also helps them to a better understanding of the period in question. The significance of historical objects lies in their genuineness, something which captivates the students both intellectually and emotionally. The Museum ensures regular information and assistance for the teachers, with the aim of having history classes in the Museum incorporated in the curricula of as many schools as possible. It sends out auxiliary material to the teachers which can be used in 5th to 8th forms of elementary schools and in secondary and apprentice training schools. To ensure close links with the schools, the Museum offers free bus fares for all Budapest students between the school and the Museum.

Another important task of the Museum in public education is its contribution to raising the cultural level of the working class and offering useful and substantial ways of spending their leisure time. Various audio-visual devices serve to turn the things seen in the exhibition into a lasting experience, by means of film-strips and slides connected with the material, texts read out from cassettes and contemporary music heard in certain sections of the exhibitions.

Saturdays and Sundays see cultural events in the Museum. The music and literary programmes linked with the exhibitions further enhance the atmosphere of a particular period, and the museum environment intensifies the mood of the programmes.

Of the Museum's periodicals, *Budapest Régiségei* (Antiquities of Budapest) was launched in 1889, and *Tanulmányok Budapest Múltjából* (Studies from the Past of Budapest) in 1932, providing regular information on the latest research result.

Miklós Horváth

DESCRIPTION
OF ILLUSTRATIONS

123 Detail of Mosaic Flooring Depicting the Myth of Hercules and Deianeira. Early 3rd century A. D.
Provenance: No. 21 Meggyfa utca, 3rd District
380 × 430 cm
The hero takes aim with his bow at the centaur Nessus, who is fleeing over the river with the wife of Hercules in his arms; beside him is the figure of Euanos, a god of the rivers. Deianeira beckons in distress to Hercules. The mosaic decorated a building in the northern quarter of the Aquincum military camp. The neighbouring hall also re-presents the figure of Hercules. The style refers the mosaics to the early third century; it was presumably prepared for the visit of Emperor Caracalla to Aquincum in A. D. 214. The mosaic flooring in the bath wing of the building depicted pugilists. The valuable mosaics are displayed in the Historical Museum's exhibition in the Hercules Villa.

124 Silver-gilt Belt Buckle. From the period of the Hungarian Conquest (10th century).
Provenance: Vöröshadsereg útja, Pestlőrinc.
Length: 5.3 cm, width: 1.95 cm

Belt buckle cast of silver. It is decorated with a carefully punched foliated scroll pattern executed in the style of the sabretache plates. The indented background protruding as a spine along its centre line is richly gilt. On the buckle's reverse there are five rivets which were simultaneously cast and their tips hammered flat. They were meant to fasten the buckle's backplate made of copper which has become highly oxidized and defective by now. On the obverse of the buckle some tiny casting defects are noticeable, and the space between the scrolls has, in fact, become perforated at several places.
Length: 5.3 cm, width: 1.95 cm

125 Silver-gilt Pair of Brooches.
Early 6th century
Part of finds excavated under the main entrance to the Roman military amphitheatre at Nagyszombat utca, Óbuda
13.6 cm, 12.1 cm
Cast silver-gilt clasps. The bow is decorated with seven silver knobs, which were attached subsequently. The surface of the bow and the pin, and both sides of the spring are covered with engraved scrollwork against a richly gilded background. The silver edges of the brooches are inlaid with niello with a zigzag pattern. At the meeting-point of the spring and the pin, and at the end of the pin are stylized animal heads. The brooches are much worn and must have been buried after long use. The knobs are missing from one of them, the iron catchplate and the pin fixed to the back are deficient on both pieces. The first letters of the German rune alphabet are engraved on the backplate of one of them. The pair of brooches might have belonged to a minor eastern German, Suebian or Herul prince.

126 White Madonna. Mid-15th century
Limestone, 89 × 24 × 31 cm
The most beautiful, most sensitively carved specimen from the sculpture gallery excavated in Buda. The trunk of the torso was found in two pieces in 1974, the head came to light at a more remote site, in 1979. The most important work of the former royal sculptor's workshop in Buda.

127 Large Figure of Knight Wearing a Belt with a Design of Daisies.
Mid-15th century
Limestone
A torso of the period that is relatively intact. The knight is shown bare-headed. One can presume a relationship between it and the figure of a herald with a similar decorative belt, which stands beside it.
Height: 135 cm and 81 cm respectively
The herald has a laurel wreath on his head, and in his hands the helmet (blazon) of a knight—presumably the one who is wearing the weapon belt in the same design.

128 Knight with Capuccio.
Mid-15th century
Limestone, 24 × 26 × 34 cm
The white limestone head with its noble features might have decorated one of the halls of the New Palace. It is the work of one of the most important masters of the fourteenth to fifteenth-century workshop, whose work shows South German influence.

129 Head of a Prophet in Hood.
Early 15th century
Limestone, 17 × 16 × 11 cm
One of the most three-dimensional types of head in the Gothic sculpture find.

130 Ornamental Sculpture from the Óbuda Provostal Church (perhaps a detail of a rood-screen).
First half of 13th century
Red marble, 68 × 35 × 16 cm
The marble is decorated with the figure of a running dog attacked by an eagle, among richly coiling tendrils. This piece from the royal workshop comes from the provostal church of Óbuda, which was destroyed during the Mongol Invasion. Under the reign of King Matthias Corvinus, the ruins of the church were demolished and the stones used for new buildings. This piece was used for the walls of today's Királyfürdő baths, taken there as part of the building material from the ruins of medieval houses that were destroyed during the Turkish occupation. During the restoration of the baths, the stone was removed from the wall brought to the Museum.

131 Carving Decorated with a Dragon.
End of 15th century
Marble, 80 × 54.5 × 15 cm
The carving has come down to us from one of the Renaissance halls of the former Royal Palace in Buda. The shaping of the dragon shows affinity with a relief from Verrocchio's workshop. It might have been carved under its influence in the workshop of the Buda palace, which employed many Italian masters. The building operations were headed for several years by the sculptor Giovanni Dalmata, who was richly rewarded for his activity by King Matthias Corvinus. The piece was found during the excavations which were started in 1947.

132 Coat of Arms of King Matthias Corvinus. Mid-15th century
Red marble, 48.3 × 44.5 × 20 cm
One of the stone coats of arms that ornamented the Buda palace, decorated with the type of heraldic device that often features on King Matthias Corvinus's coins. In the quartered shield the Czech lion also features alongside the bands representing Hungary. King Matthias Corvinus's family coat of arms with a raven is in the escutcheon in the middle.

133 Fragment of Frieze with Dolphin.
End of 15th century
Red marble, 80 × 68 × 31 cm
Detail of a red marble frieze. Among the tendrils the figure of a dolphin can be seen. The dolphin was a popular animal in Italian Renaissance art. It might have been made for one of the ornate halls of King Matthias Corvinus's Buda palace, presumably being the work of an Italian master.

134 Fragment of Stove Tile with Fiddler. End of 15th century
30.5 × 12 × 2.5 cm
Alongside the ornate red marble fireplaces there might have been stoves with coloured glazed tiles in the Buda palace during the reign of King Matthias Corvinus. The historian Antonio Bonfini gives a detailed eyewitness account on them in his description of the Buda palace. The pottery making the tiles adopted the use of white tin glaze from the Hungarian maiolica workshop which worked under Italian masters. The fragment is decorated with the figure of a fiddler, attesting to the musical culture at the Buda court.

135 Stove Tile with the Figure of King Matthias Corvinus. End of 15th century
41 × 25 × 8.5 cm
This specimen was part of a tiled stove in one of the halls of the Buda palace at the time of King Matthias Corvinus. The tile was made in the Buda workshop, with mixed-glazed cover, and shows the king sitting on his throne. It was found during the excavations at the site of the Buda palace of modern times that was destroyed in the Second World War. The broken parts have been reconstructed after tile fragments with identical decorations.

136 Detail of the Sarcophagus of St Paul the Hermit. 1486
Marble, 26.6 × 35 × 10.5 cm
The tomb of St Paul the Hermit, made between 1486 and 1492 and decorated with scenes from the saint's life, was found in Budaszentlőrinc among the remnants of the monastery of the Order of St Paul, the only religious order of Hungarian origin, founded in 1300. The surviving fragment represents parts of two scenes divided by a Gothic finial: the more intact piece on the left shows two angels carrying the soul of the founder of the order to heaven. This masterpiece of Hungarian late Gothic stone carving is one of the rare pieces the name of whose maker has survived: it is the work of the Paulite stone-cutter Dénes. According to G. Gyöngyösi, the historian of the Paulites, upon seeing the beauty of the tomb a Turkish emissary to Hungary exclaimed, "He was really taught by God Almighty, not by man."

137 Stove Tile with Dragon (fragment).
End of 15th century
24.5 × 25 × 5.5 cm
The tile was part of a stove in the Angevin wing of the Buda palace, which presumably included several more tiles decorated with animal figures. The figure of the dragon is worked out with great exactitude,

and shows the high standard of the pottery workshop at the Buda palace. The dragon often features in medieval art.

138 Renaissance-style Maiolica Flooring. End of 15th century
80 × 100 cm

The flooring covered one of the halls of the Buda palace of King Matthias Corvinus's time; the pieces represent emblems of King Matthias and Queen Beatrice, vegetal ornaments and animal figures. Tiles with the initial of Matthias's name and decorated with his family coat of arms were also made for the palace. They were made in the maiolica workshop set up in the palace by Italian craftsmen from Faenza. The King also presented maiolica tiles for the palaces of his barons and prelates.

139 Console Decorated with a Girl's Head. *c.* 1360–70
Limestone, 17 × 12 × 17 cm

The console was found during the excavations in Buda Castle between 1948 and 1952. The charming head with her gentle smile presumably came from the workshop of Master János who worked on the construction of the palace. The head's connection with the Gothic sculptures excavated in 1974 is problematical, as the statues are dated to the years 1390 to 1420, while this beautiful piece, one of the finest relics of the Gothic period of Buda, is ascribed to 1360–70.

140 JÁNOS FÜLÖP BINDER
(Buda engraver, 1735?–1811):
Statue of St Philip Neri with the Zichy Mansion in Óbuda
Etching, 16.5 × 10.6 cm

The main theme of the picture is the group of statues at the right side of the votive altar made by Károly Bebó between 1758 and 1763. As borne out by the inscription under the depiction, the altar was commissioned by Erzsébet Berényi, the widow of Miklós Zichy, and it represents the patron saints against fire, the plague and earthquake: St Florian, St Charles Borromeo and St Philip Neri. The original provenance of the statue is unknown, but from 1819 onwards it was standing in Fló-

rián tér in Óbuda, and it was removed during the construction work of nearby Árpád Bridge. The etching shows the Danube in the foreground with an arrow indicating the direction of its flow, and with a boat and a ship with a water-mill. The Zichy mansion in Óbuda is seen on the right bank. To the left a group of buildings of the Trinitarian monastery and church of Kiscell merge into the landscape in the background.

141 FISCHER VON ERLACH (b. 1656, Graz–d. 1723, Vienna) and BENJAMIN KENCKEL (engraver active in the early 18th century):
Picture of the Turkish Mosque in Pest
Engraving, 29 × 42.4 cm

The Pest mosque was represented on the same plate with the one in Bursa. The inscription under the Pest picture reads: "Türkische Mosquéé so zu Pest zusehen. Mosquéé qui est à Pest en Hongrie". Up till 1735, the mosque with its minaret stood on the plot of the House of the Invalids in the city of Pest. The original drawing is in Fischer von Erlach's manuscript which he finished in 1712, preserved in the Vienna Nationalbibliothek. The figure of a man in the forefront was based on a drawing by Caspar Luyken, published in Nuremberg in 1703.

The inscription under the Bursa mosque reads: "J.B.F.v.E: del – C:P.S.C:M-Gravé par B".

Published in Fischer von Erlach: *Entwurff einer historischen Architektur . . .*, in 1726.

142 Stemmed Glass.
Second half on 19th century
8.8 × 7.7 × 16 cm

An uncoloured goblet of thick glass and smooth surface, with painted decoration. The cylindrical cup is rounded off at the bottom. The oblong painting in a brown tone on the side, framed with two lines, a thick white and a thin dark brown, presents the Chain Bridge from its Pest end, with the slope of Castle Hill covered with trees, in the background. The inscription reads: "Kettenbrücke zwischen Pest u. Ofen". The opposite side is decorated with scarcely visible, scattered white flowers. The stem and the strongly convex base are smooth.

143 Goblet with Lid.
Second half of 19th century
32.5 × 9 × 9.9 cm
A thin-walled, uncoloured, stemmed goblet of blown and cut glass with ground surface. The cup widens upwards, on one side is the engraved picture of the Chain Bridge from its Buda end, in a square field with curved sides, framed with a ground line, with the picture of the Pest embankment of the Danube in the background. The inscription in Gothic letters reads "Pesth".

The floral ornament on the other side shows Hungarian taste. The smoothly ground stem is divided into discs, the circular base is decorated with ground Hungarian pattern. The grinding on the protruding circular lid is similar to that on the foot. The haft of the lid is divided into discs and terminates in a knob.

144 MIKLÓS BARABÁS
(b. 1810, Márkusfalva [now Markušovce, Czechoslovakia]–d. 1898, Budapest):
The Lower Danube Embankment at Pest. 1843
Water-colour on paper, 22.5 × 31.5 cm
The picture of the lower Danube embankment at Pest seen from the south, with the Serbian Church, the Municipal Concert Hall (Vigadó) built by Mihály Pollack, and the row of palaces along the riverside. The market scene on the embankment shows peasant women selling bread, carts, and a couple in middle-class garments, walking arm in arm in the foreground. Ships are moored side by side along the Pest bank. A pontoon bridge crosses the Danube. To the left the Castle and the hazy, blurred outlines of the Buda hills can be seen in the background.

145 ANTAL LIGETI (b. 1823, Nagykároly [now Carei, Rumania]–d. 1890, Budapest):
Buda and Pest. 1887
Oil on canvas, 100 × 151 cm

Ligeti sketched out the picture in 1864 and worked it up in 1887. The landscape is seen from today's Boráros tér. On the left are the Gellért Hill, the Castle Hill and the Chain Bridge, with more Buda hills in the background.

The genre-scene in the forefront depicts horses resting, people moving about, and boats, ships and barges in the Danube.

To the right the city of Pest appears along the bank forming a bay.

146 MÓR ERDÉLYI (1877–1929):
Tabán Street Scene. c. 1910
Photograph, 17 × 19 cm
The photograph was taken in the Tabán quarter which was pulled down in the 1930s, and presents a section of Hadnagy utca leading from Döbrentei tér to Hegyalja út. The photograph depicting one of the typical streets of the Tabán, which has often been immortalized by writers and painters, is one of a series of photographs of the quarter by Mór Erdélyi.

147 GYÖRGY KLÖSZ (1844–1913):
Gizella (Vörösmarty) tér. c. 1890
Photograph, 24 × 30 cm
The photograph shows the one-time Gizella (today Vörösmarty) tér in Pest. A hackney-carriage stands in the middle of the picture, with the former Magyar Király (Hungarian King) Hotel in Dorottya utca to the left, and the building of the Pest Hungarian Commercial Bank over the square.

148 GYÖRGY KLÖSZ (1844–1913):
Városház tér in Pest. c. 1890
Photograph, 24 × 30 cm
The photograph shows the northern side of Városház (Town Hall) tér, which formed the centre of the old city of Pest and was demolished during the construction work of Elizabeth Bridge; today it is Pesti Barnabás utca. The square was the trading centre of the city. The photograph shows bustling traffic, with carts, hackney-carriages and horse-drawn vehicles.

1 (a–c) Urns from Center.
20th century B.C. Clay

2 Cart vessel from
Budakalász. End of 3rd
millennium B.C. Burnt clay

3 Scythian gold stags.
(a) Gold stag from
Zöldhalompuszta. Second
half of 6th century B.C. Gold
(b) Gold stag from
Tápiószentmárton.
Electrum

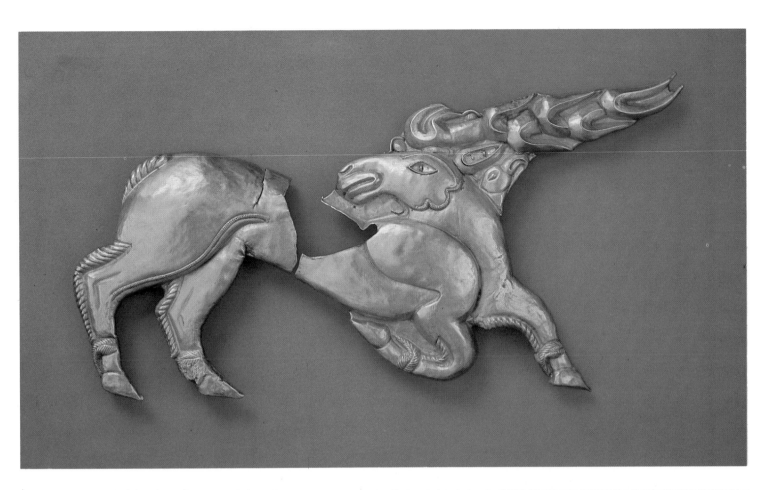

4 (a-b) Bronze jug and
patera. 1st century B.C.
Bronze and copper

5 Glass cup with reticulated
ornament. Might have come
to Pannonia in the early 4th
century A.D. Early Christian
relic

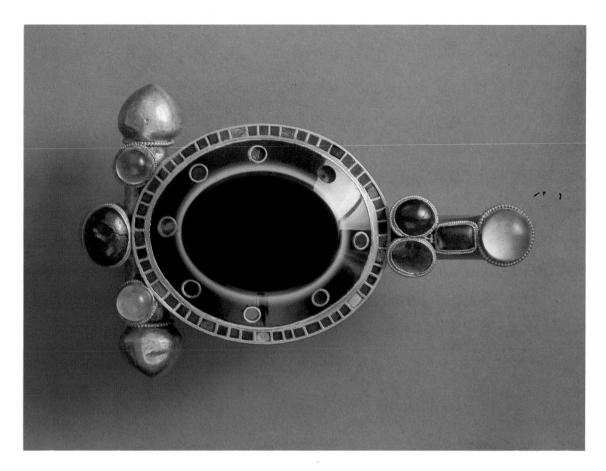

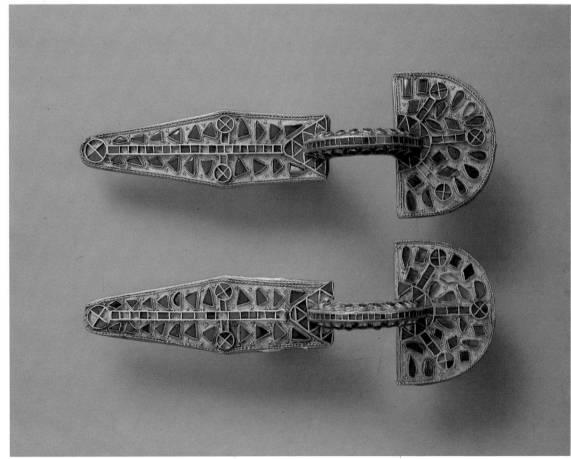

6 Late Roman ornate helmet. Second half of 4th century A.D.

7 Gold brooches from the second Szilágysomlyó hoard. End of 4th century–early 5th century A.D.
(a) Onyx gold brooch
(b) Gold brooch with knob

8 Bronze cauldron from
Törtel. End of 4th
century–early 5th century
A.D.

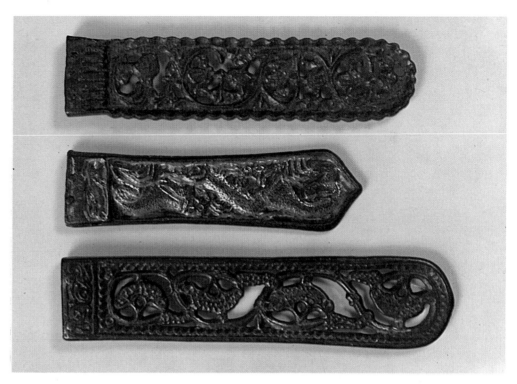

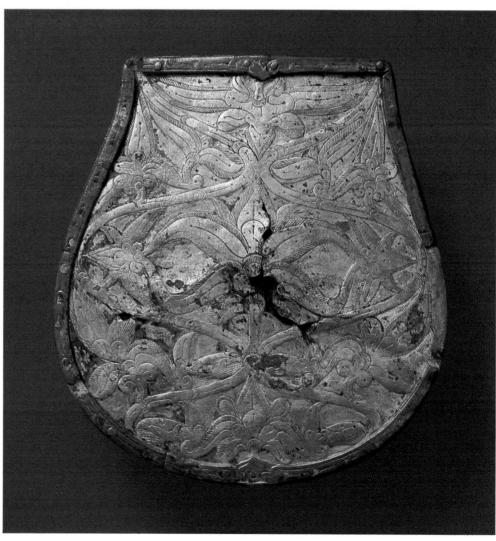

9 Avar strap-ends.
(a) Strap-end with floral
patterns. Bronze
(b) Strap-end with animal
combat. Bronze
(c) Strap-end with vegetal
ornament. Bronze

10 Sabretache plate from
Tarcal. 10th century. Silver,
copper

11 Crown of Byzantine
Emperor Constantine IX
Monomachus. Nyitraivánka
(now Ivanka pri Nitra,
Czechoslovakia).
Between 1042 and 1050.
Bronze, *cloisonné* enamel
(a) Monomachus Crown—
detail, with the picture of the
Emperor

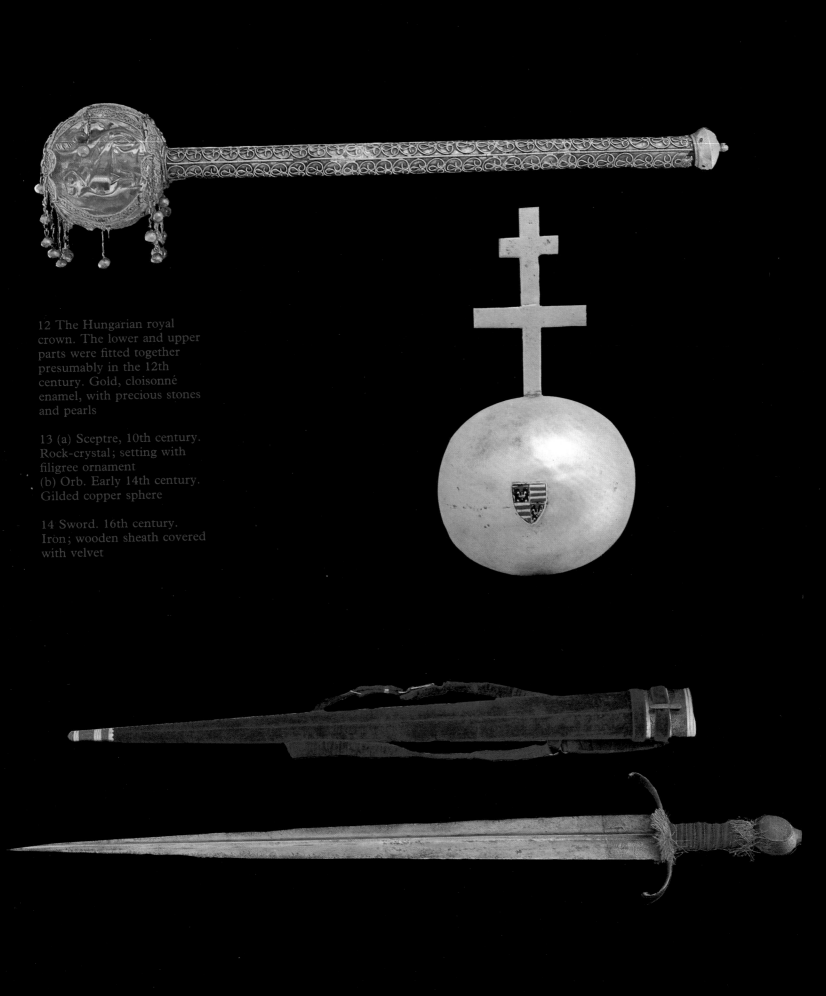

12 The Hungarian royal
crown. The lower and upper
parts were fitted together
presumably in the 12th
century. Gold, cloisonné
enamel, with precious stones
and pearls

13 (a) Sceptre, 10th century.
Rock-crystal; setting with
filigree ornament
(b) Orb. Early 14th century.
Gilded copper sphere

14 Sword. 16th century.
Iron; wooden sheath covered
with velvet

15 Coronation mantle. 1031. Embroidered in gold and silk thread

16 Aquamanile. 13th century.
Copper

17 Head reliquary. 14th
century. Gilded copper

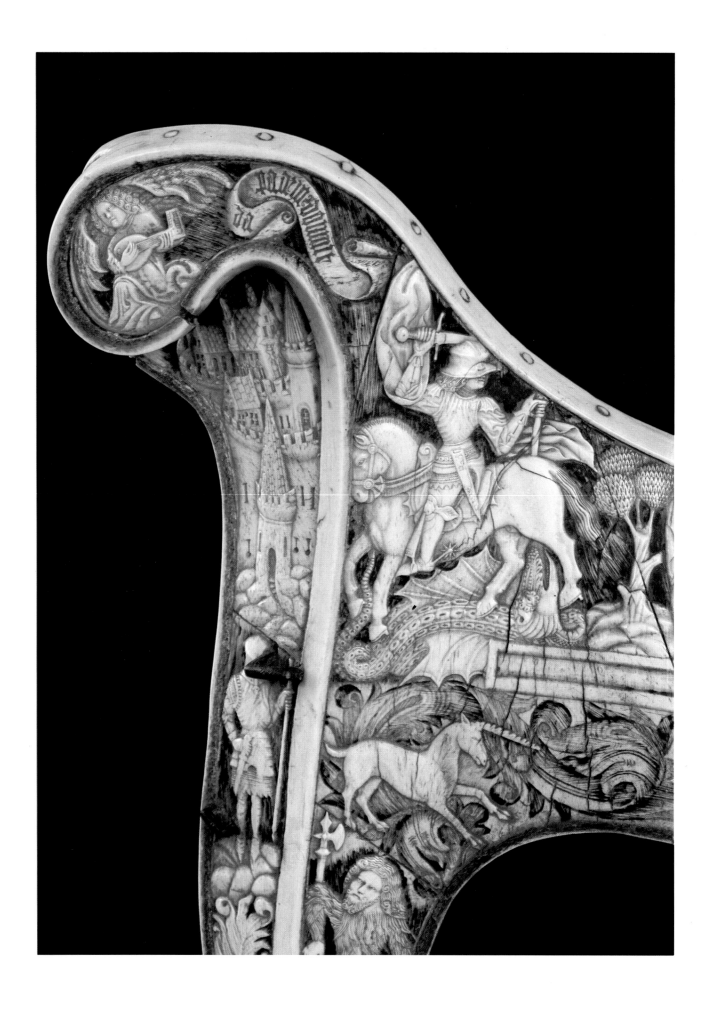

18 Bone saddle (detail). End
of 14th century–early 15th
century

19 Gothic chalice. 15th
century. Silver gilt

20 Glass goblet of King
Matthias Corvinus. Second
half of 15th century. White
striped glass; silver gilt

21 King Matthias Corvinus's
throne tapestry. 1470s. Gold
brocade

22 Ornamental papal sword
of King Wladislas II.1509.
Silver gilt

23 Ornamental weapons.
(a) Pointed dagger. 16th century. Silver-gilt sheath
(b) Sabre. 17th century. Sheath covered wit red velvet

24 Pálffy goblet with cover. Győr, 1598. Gold with coloured enamelling

25 View of the Hungarian
National Museum.
Colour lithograph by Franz
Xaver Sandmann after
a drawing by Rudolf Alt

26 Man's portrait.
Limestone. Egypt, New
Kingdom. 19th dynasty.
c. 1200 B.C.

27 Niobid. Terracotta.
2nd century B.C.

28 Athenian stele. Marble.
c. 330 B.C.

29 Gentile Bellini: The Portrait of Caterina Cornaro, Queen of Cyprus. *c.* 1500. Oil on poplar

30 Michele Pannonio: Muse Thalia. 1450–60. Tempera, oil on poplar

31 Raphael: The "Esterházy Madonna". *c.* 1508. Tempera, oil on poplar

32 Giovanni Antonio Boltraffio: Virgin and Child. Late 15th century. Oil on poplar

33 Giorgione (Giorgio da Castelfranco): Portrait of a Youth (Antonio Broccardo?). No date. Oil on canvas

34 Albrecht Dürer: Portrait of a Man (Endres Dürer). No date. Oil on pine

35 Barend van Orley: Portrait of Emperor Charles V. Late 1510s. Oil on oak

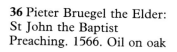

36 Pieter Bruegel the Elder:
St John the Baptist
Preaching. 1566. Oil on oak

37 Giovanni Battista Tiepolo:
St James the Greater
Conquers the Moors.
1767–69. Oil on canvas

38 Jan van Goyen: Seascape
with Fishermen. No date.
Oil on canvas

39 Johannes Vermeer van Delft:
Portrait of a Woman.
1655–60. Oil on canvas

40 El Greco: Study of a Man
(Self-portrait?).*c.* 1590.
Oil on canvas

41 Francisco de Goya: The
Water-seller (La aguadora).
Before 1812. Oil on canvas

42 Diego Velázquez: Peasants
at Table (El almuerzo).
c. 1617–18. Oil on canvas

43 Claude Monet: Fishing
Boats. 1886. Oil on canvas

44 Édouard Manet: Lady
with Fan. 1864.
Oil on canvas

45 Henri de Toulouse-Lautrec:
Ces Dames! 1894. Pastel
crayon on cardboard

46 Vincent van Gogh:
Provençal Haystack. 1888.
India ink and pen

47 Oskar Kokoschka:
Veronica. 1911. Oil on canvas

48 Marc Chagall: Blue
Village. 1968. Gouache

49 Pablo Picasso: Mother and
Child. *c.* 1905. India ink and
water-colour

50 (a) Statue of St Dorothy
from Barka (now Bôrka,
Czechoslovakia). 1410–20.
Lime, with traces of paint
(b) Upper Hungarian
Sculptor: King Saint
Stephen. *c.* 1500–10.
Limewood

51 Master M.S.:
The Visitation. 1506.
Tempera on wood

52 Madonna with Rose from
Kassa (now Košice,
Czechoslovakia). *c*. tempera
on wood and decorated gold plates

53 Jakab Bogdány: Flower
Piece. 1690s. Oil on canvas

54 Ádám Mányoki:
Self-portrait. 1700–02.
Oil on canvas

55 Károly Markó the Elder:
Visegrád. 1826–30.
Oil on canvas

56 Miklós Barabás: Portrait
of Mme Bittó. 1874.
Oil on canvas

57 Bertalan Székely:
Red-haired Girl. 1870s.
Oil on canvas

58 István Ferenczy:
Shepherdess. 1822. Marble

59 Miklós Izsó: Dancing
Peasant. 1870–71. Terracotta

60 László Mednyánszky:
Head of a Tramp. 1897.
Oil on canvas

61 Mihály Munkácsy: Dusty
Road. 1874. Oil on wood

62 Pál Szinyei Merse: Picnic
in May. 1873. Oil on canvas

63 Károly Ferenczy: October.
1903. Oil on canvas

64 Aladár Körösfői-Kriesch: Study for Klára Zách. 1912. Pastel on paper

65 Lajos Gulácsy: Paolo and Francesca. 1903. Pencil and water-colour on paper

66 József Rippl-Rónai:
Father and Uncle Piacsek
Drinking Red Wine. 1907.
Oil and crayon on cardboard

67 Lajos Tihanyi: Portrait of
Lajos Fülep. 1915.
Oil on canvas

68 Tivadar Csontváry Kosztka:
Ruins of the Greek Theatre at Taormina. 1904–05. Oil on canvas

69 József Nemes Lampérth:
Female Nude from the Back.
1916. Oil on canvas

70 József Egry: Badacsony
Lights (Golden Gate).
1943–44. Tempera and pastel
on paper

71 Gyula Derkovits: Mother. 1934. Tempera on canvas

72 Béla Kondor: The Genius of Mechanical Flight. 1964. Oil on canvas

73 Shaka Nyorai: Buddha.
"Dry Lacquer" statue. 8th
century

74 (a-b) Genji Album. Tosa
School. 17th century.
Coloured miniature paintings
on paper with golden
ornamentation

75 Chi Pay-shi: Bamboo.
Late 1920s – early 1930s.
Painted on paper with black
India ink, mounted on
a scroll, with silk brocade
frame

76 Chi Pay-shi: Autumn
Fragrance, Autumn Hue.
1948. Painted on paper with
India ink and colours.
A kakemono

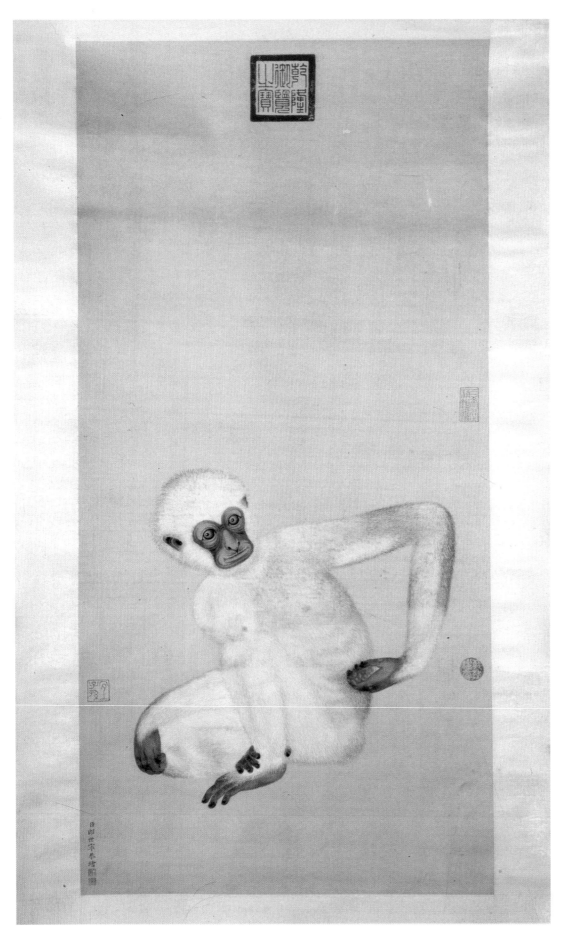

77 Lang Shi-ning: White
Monkey. 17th–18th century.
Water-colour, scroll on silk
and mounted on paper

78 (a) *Cloisonné* enamel vase.
Mid-15th century
(b) *Cloisonné* enamel wall
vase. 18th century

79 (a) Comb with case.
17th century. Horn with gold
case
(b) Sword hilt.
17th century

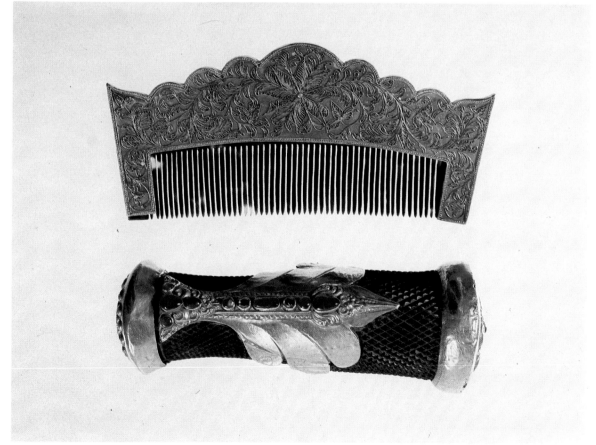

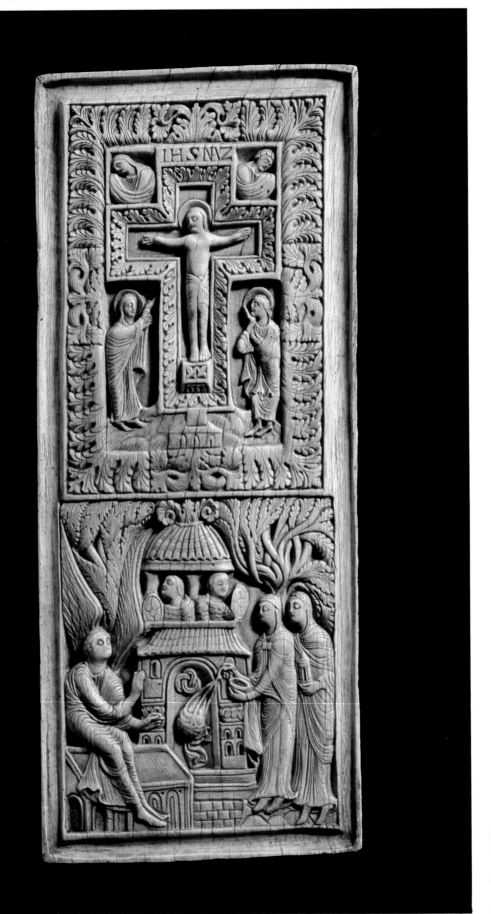

80 Book plate. St Gallen.
c. 900. Ivory, flat carving

81 Book cover. Transylvania.
1629. Light brown gilded
leather

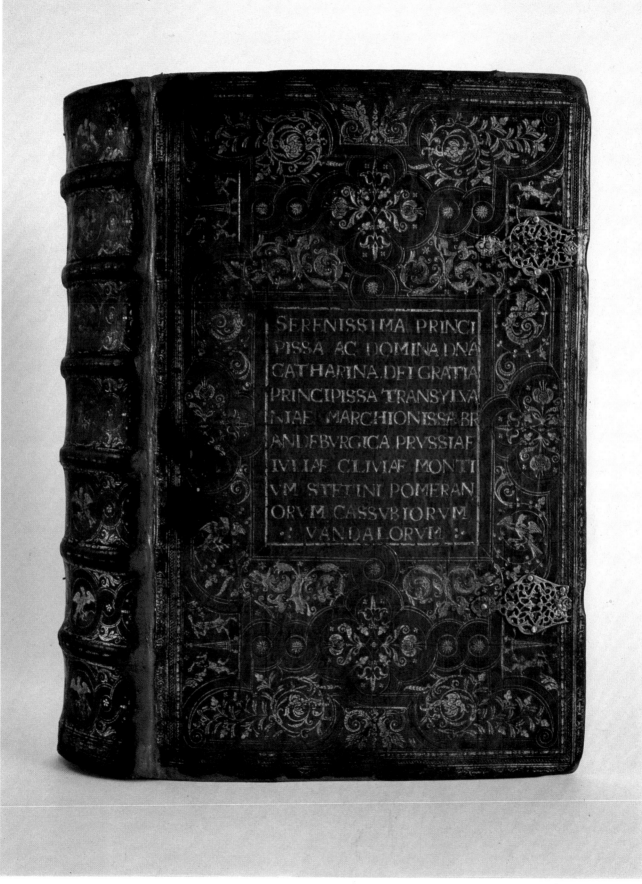

SERENISSIMA PRINCI
PISSA AC DOMINA DNA
CATHARINA DEI GRATIA
PRINCIPISSA TRANSYLVA
NIAE MARCHIONISSAE BR
ANDEBVRGICA PRVSSIAE
IVLIAE CLIVIAE MONTI
VM STETINI POMERAN
ORVM CASSVBIORVM
:· VANDALORVM ·:

82 Tapestry (the "Győr
Tapestry"). Brussels. *c.* 1520.
Coloured wool, woven of silk
and gold threads

83 Chasuble. Early 16th century. Hungarian embroidery on Venetian velvet brocade

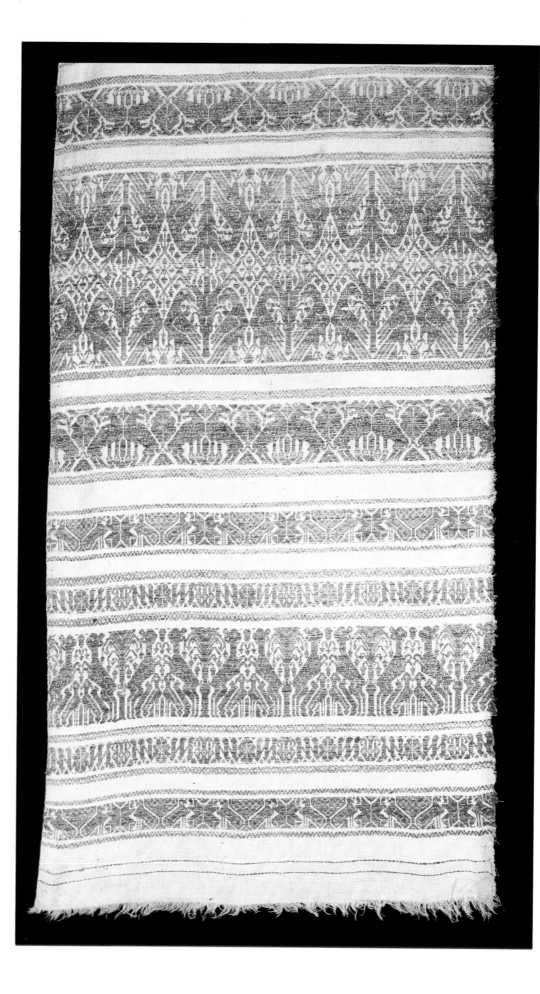

84 Rug. Usak (Anatolia, Asia Minor). 17th century. Knotted of coloured wool

85 Table-cloth. Upper Hungary (now Czechoslovakia). 17th century. Linen cloth with blue cotton woven pattern

86 The Holy Family.
1500–50. Boxwood carving.
German work

87 St John. *c.* 1500 Boxwood
carving. Flemish work

88 Icon. Cretan-Venetian circle. 17th century. Painted on a panel against a gilded background

89 Goblet with cover (the so-called "Szapolyai Goblet"). Nuremberg. *c.* 1520. Signed

90 Triton and Amphitrite. *c.* 1600. Gold, with enamel, jewels and pearls

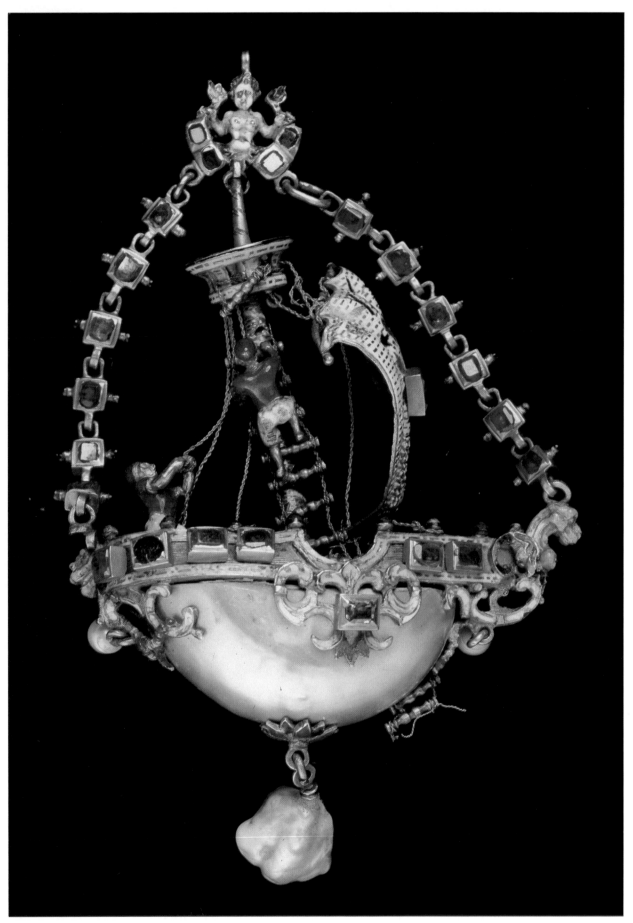

91 Amor's ship. 17th century. Gold with *champlevé* and *ronde bosse* enamel, rubies and diamonds

92 Jug. German (Kreussen).
17th century. Stoneware with
protuberant ornamentation,
a pewter lid and oil enamel
painting

93 Mantelpiece clock. Paris.
Early 19th century. Guilded
bronze on marble pedestal

94 Haban dish. 1695.
With IS initials. Northern
Hungary. White tin-glazed
faience, painted with metallic
oxide paints

95 Honeycake mould. Kassa
(now Košice, Czechoslovakia). 1631.
With MS initials.
Walnut, with hollowed-out carving

96 Antoine Criaerd: Commode. *c.* 1740.
With rosewood veneer,
palisander marquetry and
bronze studs

97 L. C. Tiffany:
Vase and goblet. *c.* 1900.
Polychromatic iridescent and
opalesque glass

98 József Rippl-Rónai:
Woman in Red. 1898.
Embroidered wall hanging

99 Pharmacy furniture
(detail). 1744. Oak, in places
with walnut veneer and
carved carved details

100 Ostyak fur bag. Sosva region, Siberia.

101 Poison cup.
Congo. Bewongo.
Dark brown wood

102 Shaman's mantle.
Mongolia. 19th–20th century.
Blue linen cloth

103 Dance mask.
19th century. Liberia. Brown
wood painted black

104 Statue. Veracruz,
Mexico. Reddish-brown clay.
Copy of a clay model from
the 1st–6th centuries A.D.

105 Beehive. 19th century.
Nőtincs, Nógrád County.
Limewood, covered with
a liuden board

106 Salt-cellar. 1891.
Lengyeltóti, Somogy County.
An oval box of horn with
wooden bottom and lid

107 Powder-horn.
18th century. Magyarszákos
(now Sacoşul rom, Rumania).
Cut from antlers

108 Scab-grease holder. 1914.
Trans-Tisza region.
Lid carved from ox-horn

109 Mirror-case. 1840.
Magyargencs, Vas County.
Hardwood

110 Razor case. 19th century.
Ormánság. Baranya County
Hardwood

111 Stove tile. Alsópáhok,
Zala County

112 Mirror. 19th century.
Hódmezővásárhely,
Csongrád County. Pine

113 Chair. 1837. Kóny,
Győr-Sopron County.
Walnut and oak

114 Church chest. Rozsonda
(now Ruja, Rumania).
Beech-wood

115 Chest. 19th century.
Decs, Tolna County. Pine

116 Drinking vessel. 19th century. Magyarhegymeg (now Uhorské, Czechoslovakia). Hard wood

117 Dish. 1780. Great Hungarian Plain. Thrown lead-glazed fired clay

118 Bonnet. 19th century. Laskó (now Lug, Yugoslavia). Black linen

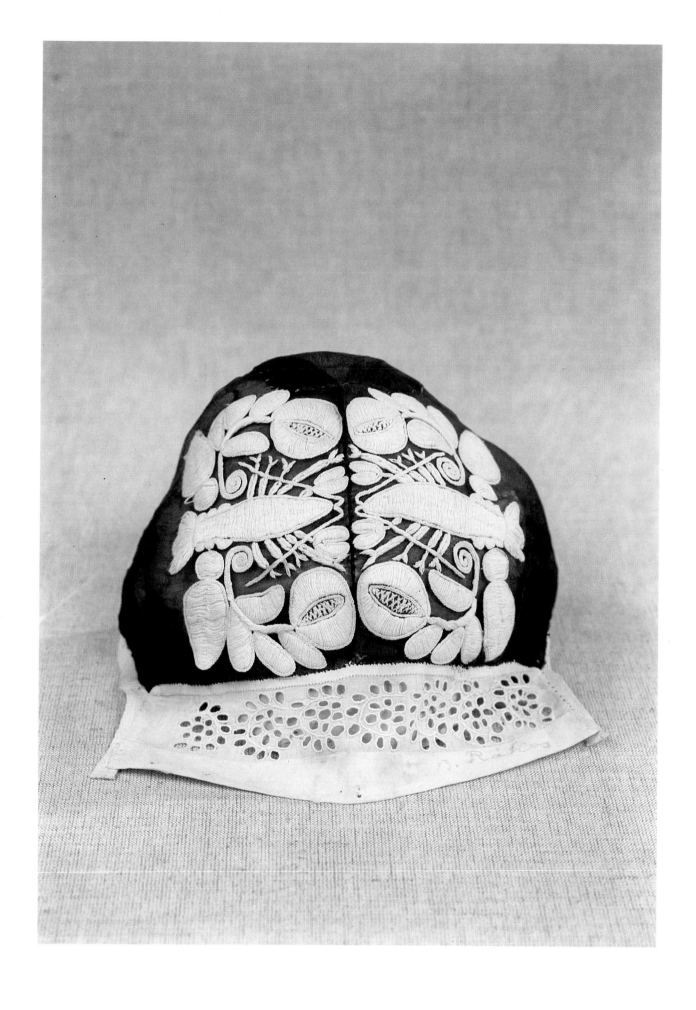

119 *Szűr* (felt cloak). 1883.
Somogy County. Of white
felt with appliqué and
embroidery

120 *Ködmön* (jacket).
19th century. Mezőkövesd,
Borsod-Abaúj-Zemplén
County. Sheepskin with
white, red and green leather
appliqué work

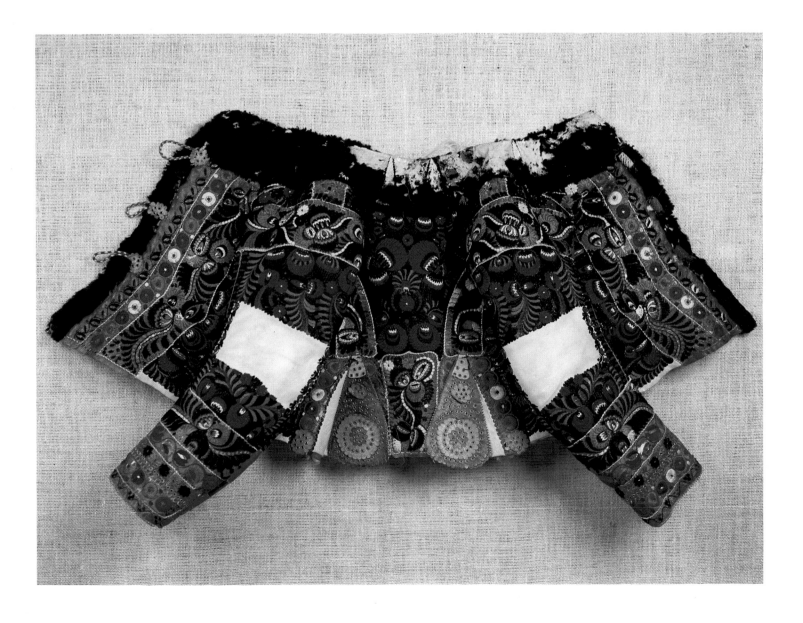

121 Big jug. 1744.
Vörösberény, Veszprém
County. Thrown lead-glazed
fired clay

122 Bottle. 1879. Tiszafüred,
Szolnok County

123 Detail of mosaic flooring depicting a mythological scene. Early 3rd century A. D.

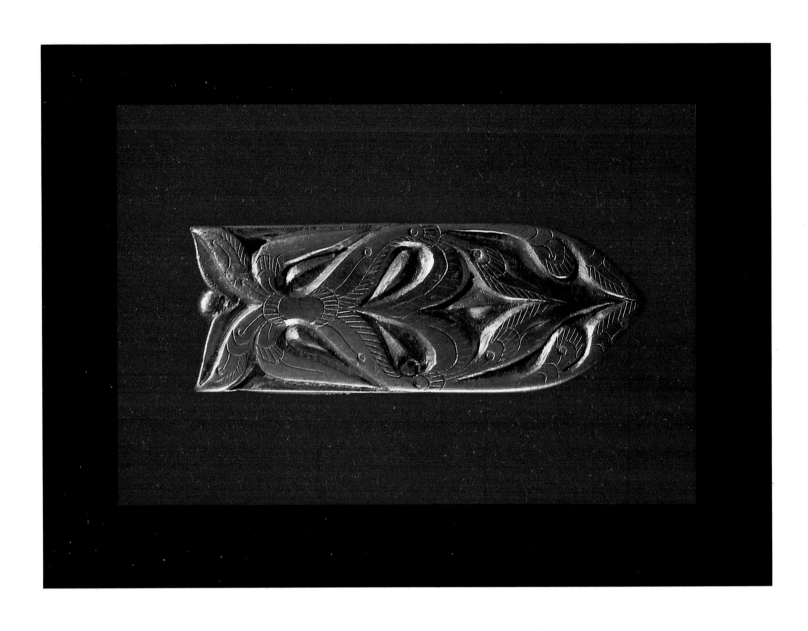

124 Silver-gilt belt buckle.
10th century

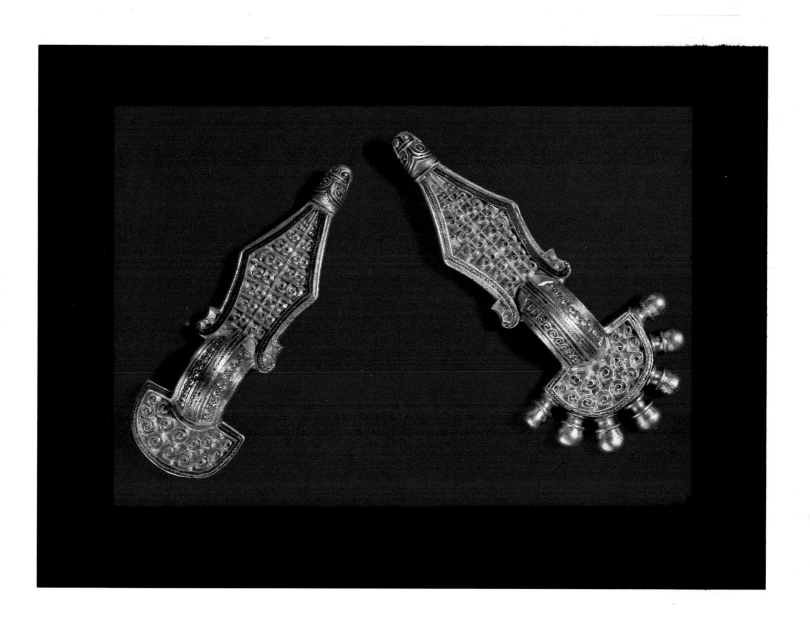

125 Silver-gilt pair of
brooches. Early 6th century

126 White Madonna.
Mid-15th century. Limestone

127 Large figure of knight
wearing a belt with a design
of daisies. Herald with
a similar decorative belt.
Mid-15th century. Limestone

128 Knight with capuccio. Mid-15th century. Limestone

129 Head of a prophet in hood. Early 15th century. Limestone

130 Ornamental sculpture
from the Óbuda provostal
church. First half of 13th
century. Red marble

131 Carving decorated with
dragon. End of 15th century.
Marble

132 Coat of arms of King Matthias Corvinus. Mid-15th century. Red marble

133 Fragment of frieze with dolphin. End of 15th century. Red marble

134 Fragment of stove tile with fiddler from the Buda palace. End of 15th century

135 Stove tile with the figure of King Matthias Corvinus from the Buda palace. End of 15th century

136 Detail of the sarcophagus
of St Paul the Hermit. 1486.
Marble

137 Stove tile with dragon (fragment). End of 15th century

138 Renaissance-style maiolica flooring from the Buda palace. End of 15th century

139 Console decorated with a girl's head. *c.* 1360–70. Limestone

Joh. Phil. Binder Sc. Bud æ.

Alt Ofnerisches denckmahl, so Gott und der Gedächtnus seines H. Philippi Nerei, im 1763ten Jahr, Von wegen gnädigster Befreyung des Erdbebens aufgerichtet, Ihro Excellence Verwittwete Gräfin Zichy geb. Gräfin Berényi.

140 János Fülöp Binder:
Statue of St Philip Neri with
the Zichy mansion in Óbuda.
18th century

141 Fischer von Erlach and
Benjamin Kenckel: Picture of
the Turkish Mosque in Pest.
Early 18th century.
Engraving

Türckische Mosquée so zu
Pest zusehen.

Mosquée qui est à Pest en
Hongrie.

142 Stemmed glass. Second half of 19th century

143 Goblet with lid. Second
half of 19th century

144 Miklós Barabás: The
Lower Danube Embankment
at Pest. 1843. Water-colour
on paper

145 Antal Ligeti: Buda and
Pest. 1887. Oil on canvas

146 Mór Erdélyi: Tabán
street scene. *c.* 1910.
Photograph

147 György Klösz: Gizella
(Vörösmarty) tér. *c.* 1890.
Photograph

148 György Klösz: Városház tér in Pest. *c.* 1890. Photograph